ideas — or lack of ideas — as to what might suitably take its place. The urgency of these reflections has been sharpened by the sensational developments — disorders on the Columbia campus as well as those among students in France, Germany and elsewhere — that have occurred since the original article was prepared.

In conclusion, Mr. Kennan sets forth certain aspects of his political philosophy to which he has not previously given public expression; and he presents, by way of contrast with the students' preoccupations, his own scale of priorities in American domestic problems and his own view of those goals to which student idealism might more constructively and hopefully be addressed.

George F. Kennan has been one of America's most distinguished public servants. His recently published *Memoirs: 1925-1950* was both a National Book Award and Pulitzer Prize winner.

By George F. Kennan

AMERICAN DIPLOMACY 1900–1950
REALITIES OF AMERICAN FOREIGN POLICY
SOVIET-AMERICAN RELATIONS 1917–1920
Volume I: Russia Leaves the War
Volume II: Decision to Intervene

RUSSIA, THE ATOM AND THE WEST
SOVIET FOREIGN POLICY 1917–1941
RUSSIA AND THE WEST UNDER LENIN AND STALIN
ON DEALING WITH THE COMMUNIST WORLD
MEMOIRS: 1925–1950
DEMOCRACY AND THE STUDENT LEFT

DEMOCRACY
and the
STUDENT LEFT

DEMOCRACY
and the
STUDENT LEFT

by
GEORGE F. KENNAN
and

Students and Teachers from:

BARNARD   BRANDEIS   BROOKLYN   CALIFORNIA   COLUMBIA
CORNELL   DARTMOUTH   HARVARD   ILLINOIS INSTITUTE OF
TECHNOLOGY   MASSACHUSETTS INSTITUTE OF TECHNOLOGY
NOTRE DAME   OHIO STATE   PRINCETON   ROCHESTER   RUTGERS
SYRACUSE   TORONTO   WESLEYAN   WEST VIRGINIA
WILLIAMS   YALE

An Atlantic Monthly Press Book

Little, Brown and Company   *Boston · Toronto*

ATLANTIC–LITTLE, BROWN BOOKS
ARE PUBLISHED BY
LITTLE, BROWN AND COMPANY
IN ASSOCIATION WITH
THE ATLANTIC MONTHLY PRESS

Published simultaneously in Canada
by Little, Brown & Company (Canada) Limited

PRINTED IN THE UNITED STATES OF AMERICA

CONTENTS

viii

IV. MR. KENNAN REPLIES

PUBLISHER'S NOTE

The speech which George F. Kennan prepared for the dedication of the new library at Swarthmore College was printed under the title of "Rebels Without a Program" in the New York *Times* Sunday Magazine for January 21, 1968. It drew an unprecedented response from students and teachers on many campuses, some addressed to the editor of the *Times* and an equal number to Mr. Kennan in Princeton. We wish particularly to thank Mr. Lewis Bergman, editor of the New York *Times* Sunday Magazine, for his early encouragement of this volume.

I

REBELS WITHOUT A PROGRAM

THERE is an ideal that has long been basic to the learning process as we have known it, one that stands at the very center of our modern institutions of higher education and that had its origin, I suppose, in the clerical and monastic character of the medieval university. It is the ideal of the association of the process of learning with a certain remoteness from the contemporary scene — a certain detachment and seclusion, a certain voluntary withdrawal and renunciation of participation in contemporary life in the interests of the achievement of a better perspective on that life when the period of withdrawal is over. It is an ideal that does not predicate any total conflict between thought and action, but recognizes that there is a time for each.

No more striking, or moving, description of this ideal has ever come to my attention than that which was given by Woodrow Wilson in 1896 at the time of the Princeton Sesquicentennial.

"I have had sight," Wilson said, "of the perfect place of learning in my thought: a free place, and a various, where no man could be and not know with how great

3

a destiny knowledge had come into the world — itself a little world; but not perplexed, living with a singleness of aim not known without; the home of sagacious men, hardheaded and with a will to know, debaters of the world's questions every day and used to the rough ways of democracy; and yet a place removed — calm Science seated there, recluse, ascetic, like a nun; not knowing that the world passes, not caring, if the truth but come in answer to her prayer. . . . A place where ideals are kept in heart in an air they can breathe; but no fool's paradise. A place where to hear the truth about the past and hold debate about the affairs of the present, with knowledge and without passion; like the world in having all men's life at heart, a place for men and all that concerns them; but unlike the world in its self-possession, its thorough way of talk, its care to know more than the moment brings to light; slow to take excitement, its air pure and wholesome with a breath of faith; every eye within it bright in the clear day and quick to look toward heaven for the confirmation of its hope. Who shall show us the way to this place?"

There is a dreadful incongruity between this vision and the state of mind — and behavior — of the radical left on the American campus today. In place of a calm science, "recluse, ascetic, like a nun," not knowing or caring that the world passes "if the truth but come in answer to her prayer," we have people utterly absorbed in the affairs of this passing world. And instead of these affairs being discussed with knowledge and without passion, we find them treated with transports of passion and

4

with a minimum, I fear, of knowledge. In place of slow-ness to take excitement, we have a readiness to react emotionally, and at once, to a great variety of issues. In place of self-possession, we have screaming tantrums and brawling in the streets. In place of the "thorough way of talk" that Wilson envisaged, we have banners and epithets and obscenities and virtually meaningless slogans. And in place of bright eyes "looking to heaven for the confirmation of their hope," we have eyes glazed with anger and passion, too often dimmed as well by artificial abuse of the psychic structure that lies behind them, and looking almost everywhere else but to heaven for the satisfaction of their aspirations.

I quite understand that those who espouse this flagrant repudiation of the Wilsonian ideal constitute only a minority on any campus. But tendencies that represent the obsession of only a few may not be without partial appeal, at certain times, and within certain limits, to many others. If my own analysis is correct, there are a great many students who may resist any complete surrender to these tendencies, but who nevertheless find them intensely interesting, are to some extent attracted or morally bewildered by them, find themselves driven, in confrontation with them, either into various forms of pleasing temptation, on the one hand, or into crises of conscience, on the other.

If I see them correctly (and I have no pretensions to authority on this subject), there are two dominant tendencies among the people I have here in mind, and superficially they would seem to be in conflict one with the

5

other. On the one side there is angry militancy, full of hatred and intolerance and often quite prepared to embrace violence as a source of change. On the other side there is gentleness, passivity, quietism — ostensibly a yearning for detachment from the affairs of the world, not the detachment Woodrow Wilson had in mind, for that was one intimately and sternly related to the real world, the objective, external world, whereas this one takes the form of an attempt to escape into a world which is altogether illusory and subjective.

What strikes one first about the angry militancy is the extraordinary degree of certainty by which it is inspired: certainty of one's own rectitude, certainty of the accuracy and profundity of one's own analysis of the problems of contemporary society, certainty as to the iniquity of those who disagree. Of course, vehemence of feeling and a conviction that right is on one's side have seldom been absent from the feelings of politically excited youth. But somehow or other they seem particularly out of place at just this time. Never has there been an era when the problems of public policy even approached in their complexity those by which our society is confronted today, in this age of technical innovation and the explosion of knowledge. The understanding of these problems is something to which one could well give years of disciplined and restrained study, years of the scholar's detachment, years of readiness to reserve judgment while evidence is being accumulated. And this being so, one is struck to see such massive certainties already present in the minds of people who not only *have not* studied very much but presumably *are not* studying a great deal, because it is hard to imagine that the activities to which this aroused portion of our student population gives itself are ones readily compatible with quiet and successful study.

The world seems to be full, today, of embattled students. The public prints are seldom devoid of the record of their activities. Photographs of them may be seen daily: screaming, throwing stones, breaking windows, overturning cars, being beaten or dragged about by police and, in the case of those on other continents, burning libraries. That these people are embattled is unquestionable. That they are really students, I must be permitted to doubt. I have heard it freely confessed by members of the revolutionary student generation of Tsarist Russia that, proud as they were of the revolutionary exploits of their youth, they never really learned anything in their university years; they were too busy with politics. The fact of the matter is that the state of being *enragé* is simply incompatible with fruitful study. It implies a degree of existing emotional and intellectual commitment which leaves little room for open-minded curiosity.

I am not saying that students should not be concerned, should not have views, should not question what goes on in the field of national policy and should not voice their questions about it. Some of us, who are older, share many of their misgivings, many of their impulses. Some of us have no less lively a sense of the dangers of the time, and are no happier than they are about a great

7

many things that are now going on. But it lies within the power as well as the duty of all of us to recognize not only the possibility that we might be wrong but the virtual certainty that on some occasions we are bound to be. The fact that this is so does not absolve us from the duty of having views and putting them forward. But it does make it incumbent upon us to recognize the element of doubt that still surrounds the correctness of these views. And if we do that, we will not be able to lose ourselves in transports of moral indignation against those who are of opposite opinion and follow a different line; we will put our views forward only with a prayer for forgiveness for the event that we prove to be mistaken.

I am aware that inhibitions and restraints of this sort on the part of us older people would be attributed by many members of the student left to a sweeping corruption of our moral integrity. Life, they would hold, has impelled us to the making of compromises; and these compromises have destroyed the usefulness of our contribution. Crippled by our own cowardice, prisoners of the seamy adjustments we have made in order to be successfully a part of the American establishment, we are regarded as no longer capable of looking steadily into the strong clear light of truth.

In this, as in most of the reproaches with which our children shower us, there is of course an element of justification. There is a point somewhere along the way in most of our adult lives, admittedly, when enthusiasms flag, when idealism becomes tempered, when responsi-

8

bility to others, and even affection for others, compels greater attention to the mundane demands of private life. There is a point when we are even impelled to place the needs of children ahead of the dictates of a defiant idealism, and to devote ourselves, pusillanimously, if you will, to the support and rearing of these same children — precisely in order that at some future date they may have the privilege of turning upon us and despising us for the materialistic faintheartedness that made their maturity possible. This, no doubt, is the nature of the compromise that millions of us make with the imperfections of government and society in our time. Many of us could wish that it might have been otherwise — that the idealistic pursuit of public causes might have remained our exclusive dedication down into later life.

But for the fact that this is not so I cannot shower myself or others with reproaches. I have seen more harm done in this world by those who tried to storm the bastions of society in the name of utopian beliefs, who were determined to achieve the elimination of all evil and the realization of the millennium within their own time, than by all the humble efforts of those who have tried to create a little order and civility and affection within their own intimate entourage, even at the cost of tolerating a great deal of evil in the public domain. Behind this modesty, after all, there has been the recognition of a vitally important truth — a truth that the Marxists, among others, have never brought themselves to recognize — namely, that the decisive seat of evil in this world is not in social and political institutions, and not even, as a rule, in the will or iniquities of statesmen, but simply in the weakness and imperfection of the human soul itself, and by that I mean literally every soul, including my own and that of the student militant at the gates. For this reason, as Tocqueville so clearly perceived when he visited this country a hundred and thirty years ago, the success of a society may be said, like charity, to begin at home.

So much, then, for the angry ones. Now, a word about the others: the quiescent ones, the hippies and the flower people.

In one sense, my feeling for these people is one of pity, not unmixed, in some instances, with horror. I am sure that they want none of this pity. They would feel that it comes to them for the wrong reasons. If they feel sorry for themselves, it is because they see themselves as the victims of a harsh, hypocritical and unworthy adult society. If I feel sorry for them, it is because I see them as the victims of certain great and destructive philosophic errors.

One of these errors — and it is one that affects particularly those who take drugs, but not those alone — is the belief that the human being has marvelous resources within himself that can be released and made available to him merely by the passive submission to certain sorts of stimuli: by letting esthetic impressions of one sort or another roll over him or by letting his psychic equilibrium be disoriented by chemical agencies that give him the sensation of experiencing tremendous things. Well, it is true that human beings sometimes have marvelous resources within themselves. It is also true that these resources are capable, ideally, of being released and made available to the man that harbors them and through him to others, and sometimes are so released. But it is not true that they can be released by hippie means.

It is only through effort, through doing, through action — never through passive experience — that man grows creatively. It is only by volition and effort that he becomes fully aware of what he has in him of creativity and becomes capable of embodying it, of making it a part of himself, of communicating it to others. There is no pose more fraudulent — and students would do well to remember this when they look at each other — than that of the individual who pretends to have been exalted and rendered more impressive by his communion with some sort of inner voice whose revelations he is unable to describe or to enact. And particularly is this pose fraudulent when the means he has chosen to render himself susceptible to this alleged revelation is the deliberate disorientation of his own psychic system; for it may be said with surety that any artificial intervention of this sort — into the infinitely delicate balance that nature created in the form of man's psychic makeup — produces its own revenge, takes its own toll, proceeds at the cost of the true creative faculties and weakens rather than strengthens.

The second error I see in the outlook of these people is the belief in the possibility and validity of a total permissiveness. They are misjudging, here, the innermost nature of man's estate. There is not, and cannot be, such a thing as total freedom. The normal needs and frailties of the body, not to mention the elementary demands of the soul itself, would rule that out if nothing else did. But beyond that, any freedom *from* something implies a freedom to something. And because our reality is a complex one, in which conflicts of values are never absent, there can be no advance toward any particular objective, not even the pursuit of pleasure, that does not imply the sacrifice of other possible objectives. Freedom, for this reason, is definable only in terms of the obligations and restraints and sacrifices it accepts. It exists, as a concept, only in relationship to something else which is by definition its opposite; and that means commitment, duty, self-restraint.

Every great artist has known this. Every great philosopher has recognized it. It has lain at the basis of Judaic-Christian teaching. Tell me what framework of discipline you are prepared to accept, and I will attempt to tell you what freedom might mean for you. But if you tell me that you are prepared to accept no framework of discipline at all, then I will tell you, as Dostoevski told his readers, that you are destined to become the most unfree of men; for freedom begins only with the humble acceptance of membership in, and subordination to, a natural order of things, and it grows only with struggle, and self-discipline, and faith.

To shun the cruelty and corruption of this world is one thing. It is not always unjustifiable. Not everyone is made to endure these things. There is something to be said for the cultivation, by the right people, and in the

12

right way, of the virtues of detachment, of withdrawal, of unworldliness, of innocence and purity, if you will. That, as a phase of life, is just what Wilson was talking about. In an earlier age, those who are now the flower children and the hippies would perhaps have entered monastic life or scholarly life or both. But there, be it noted, they would very definitely have accepted a framework of discipline, and it would normally have been a very strict one. If it was a monastic order, their lives would have been devoted to the service of God and of other men, not of themselves and their senses. If it was the world of scholarship, their lives would have been devoted to the pursuit of truth, which never comes easily or without discipline and sacrifice. They would have accepted an obligation to cultivate order, not chaos; cleanliness, not filth; self-abnegation, not self-indulgence; health, not demoralization.

Now I have indicated that I pity these people, and in general I do. But sometimes I find it hard to pity them, because they themselves are sometimes so pitiless. There is, in this cultivation of an absolute freedom, and above all in the very self-destructiveness with which it often expresses itself, a selfishness, a hardheartedness, a callousness, an irresponsibility, an indifference to the feelings of others, that is its own condemnation. No one ever destroys just himself alone. Such is the network of intimacy in which every one of us is somehow embraced, that whoever destroys himself destroys to some extent others as well. Many of these people prattle about the principle of love; but their behavior betrays this principle in the most elementary way. Love — and by that I mean the receiving of love as well as the bestowal of it — is itself an obligation, and as such is incompatible with the quest for a perfect freedom. Just the cruelty to parents alone, which is implicit in much of this behavior, is destructive of the purest and most creative form of love that does exist or could exist in this mortal state.

And one would like to warn these young people that in distancing themselves so recklessly not only from the wisdom but from the feelings of parents, they are hacking at their own underpinnings — and even those of people as yet unborn. There could be no greater illusion than the belief that one can treat one's parents unfeelingly and with contempt and yet expect that own's own children will some day treat one otherwise; for such people break the golden chain of affection that binds the generations and gives continuity and meaning to life.

One cannot, therefore, on looking at these young people in all the glory of their defiant rags and hairdos, always just say, with tears in one's eyes: "There goes a tragically wayward youth, striving romantically to document his rebellion against the hypocrisies of the age." One has sometimes to say, and not without indignation: "There goes a perverted and willful and stony-hearted youth by whose destructiveness we are all, in the end, to be damaged and diminished."

These people also pose a problem in the quality of their citizenship. One thing they all seem to have in common — the angry ones as well as the quiet ones — is a complete rejection of, or indifference to, the political system of this country. The quiet ones turn their backs upon it, as though it did not concern them. The angry ones reject it by implication, insofar as they refuse to recognize the validity of its workings or to respect the discipline which, as a system of authority, it unavoidably entails.

I think there is a real error or misunderstanding here. If you accept a democratic system, this means that you are prepared to put up with those of its workings, legislative or administrative, with which you do not agree as well as with those that meet with your concurrence. This willingness to accept, in principle, the workings of a system based on the will of the majority, even when you yourself are in the minority, is simply the essence of democracy. Without it there could be no system of representative self-government at all. When you attempt to alter the workings of the system by means of violence or civil disobedience, this, it seems to me, can have only one of two implications: either you do not believe in democracy at all and consider that society ought to be governed by enlightened minorities such as the one to which you, of course, belong; or you consider that the present system is so imperfect that it is not truly representative, that it no longer serves adequately as a vehicle for the will of the majority, and that this leaves to the unsatisfied no adequate means of self-expression other than the primitive one of calling attention to themselves and their emotions by mass demonstrations and mass defiance of established authority. It is surely the latter of these two implications which we must read from the overwhelming majority of the demonstrations that have recently taken place.

I would submit that if you find a system inadequate, it is not enough simply to demonstrate indignation and anger over individual workings of it, such as the persistence of the Vietnam war, or individual situations it tolerates or fails to correct, such as the condition of the Negroes in our great cities. If one finds these conditions intolerable, and if one considers that they reflect no adequate expression either of the will of the majority or of that respect for the rights of minorities which is no less essential to the success of any democratic system, then one places upon one's self, it seems to me, the obligation of saying in what way this political system should be modified, or what should be established in the place of it, to assure that its workings would bear a better relationship to people's needs and people's feelings.

If the student left had a program of constitutional amendment or political reform — if it had proposals for the constructive adaptation of this political system to the needs of our age — if it was *this* that it was agitating for, and if its agitation took the form of reasoned argument and discussion, or even peaceful demonstration accompanied by reasoned argument and discussion — then many of us, I am sure, could view its protests with respect, and we would not shirk the obligation either to speak up in defense of institutions and national practices which we have tolerated all our lives, or to join these young people in the quest for better ones.

But when we are confronted only with violence for

16

violence's sake, and with attempts to frighten or intimidate an administration into doing things for which it can itself see neither the rationale nor the electoral mandate; when we are offered, as the only argument for change, the fact that a number of people are themselves very angry and excited; and when we are presented with a violent objection to what exists, unaccompanied by any constructive concept of what, ideally, ought to exist in its place — then we of my generation can only recognize that such behavior bears a disconcerting resemblance to phenomena we have witnessed within our own time in the origins of totalitarianism in other countries, and then we have no choice but to rally to the defense of a public authority with which we may not be in agreement but which is the only one we've got and with which, in some form or another, we cannot conceivably dispense. People should bear in mind that if this — namely noise, violence and lawlessness — is the way they are going to put their case, then many of us who are no happier than they are about some of the policies that arouse their indignation will have no choice but to place ourselves on the other side of the barricades.

These observations reflect a serious doubt whether civil disobedience has any place in a democratic society. But there is one objection I know will be offered to this view. Some people, who accept our political system, believe that they have a right to disregard it and to violate the laws that have flowed from it so long as they are prepared, as a matter of conscience, to accept the penalties established for such behavior.

I am sorry; I cannot agree. The violation of law is not, in the moral and philosophic sense, a privilege that lies offered for sale with a given price tag, like an object in a supermarket, available to anyone who has the price and is willing to pay for it. It is not like the privilege of breaking crockery in a tent at the county fair for a quarter a shot. Respect for the law is not an obligation which is exhausted or obliterated by willingness to accept the penalty for breaking it.

To hold otherwise would be to place the privilege of lawbreaking preferentially in the hands of the affluent, to make respect for law a commercial proposition rather than a civic duty and to deny any authority of law independent of the sanctions established against its violation. It would then be all right for a man to create false fire alarms or frivolously to pull the emergency cord on the train, or to do any number of other things that endangered or inconvenienced other people, provided only he was prepared to accept the penalties of so doing. Surely, lawlessness and civil disobedience cannot be condoned or tolerated on this ground; and those of us who care for the good order of society have no choice but to resist attempts at its violation, when this is their only justification.

Now, being myself a father, I am only too well aware that people of my generation cannot absolve ourselves of a heavy responsibility for the state of mind in which these young people find themselves. We are obliged to recognize here, in the myopia and the crudities of *their* extremism, the reflection of our own failings:

18

our faintheartedness and in some instances our weariness, our apathy in the face of great and obvious evils.

I am also aware that, while their methods may not be the right ones, and while their discontent may suffer in its effectiveness from the concentration on negative goals, the degree of their concern over the present state of our country and the dangers implicit in certain of its involvements is by no means exaggerated. This is a time in our national life more serious, more menacing, more crucial, than any I have ever experienced or ever hoped to experience. Not since the civil conflict of a century ago has this country, as I see it, been in such great danger; and the most excruciating aspect of this tragic state of affairs is that so much of this danger comes so largely from within, where we are giving it relatively little official attention, and so little of it comes, relatively speaking, from the swamps and jungles of Southeast Asia into which we are pouring our treasure of young blood and physical resources.

For these reasons, I do not mean to make light of the intensity of feeling by which this student left is seized. Nor do I mean to imply that people like myself can view this discontent from some sort of smug Olympian detachment, as though it were not our responsibility, as though it were not in part our own ugly and decadent face that we see in this distorted mirror. None of us could have any justification for attempting to enter into communication with these people if we did not recognize, along with the justification for their unhappiness, our own responsibility in the creation of it, and if we did

19

not accompany our appeal to them with a profession of readiness to join them, where they want us to, in the attempt to find better answers to many of these problems.

I am well aware that in approaching them in this way and in taking issue as I have with elements of their outlook and their behavior, it is primarily myself that I have committed, not them. I know that behind all the extremisms — all the philosophical errors, all the egocentricities and all the oddities of dress and deportment — we have to do here with troubled and often pathetically appealing people, acting, however wisely or unwisely, out of sincerity and idealism, out of the unwillingness to accept a meaningless life and a purposeless society.

Well, this is not the life, and not the sort of society, that many of us would like to leave behind us in this country when our work is done. How wonderful it would be, I sometimes think to myself, if we and they — experience on the one hand, strength and enthusiasm on the other — could join forces.

II

AGREEMENT AND DISSENT: RESPONSE FROM THE CAMPUS

Cambridge, Mass., January 25, 1968

Dear Mr. Kennan:

I hope that I am not being presumptuous in writing this letter. I am a freshman at Harvard and I plan to major in international relations. I have read several of your books, along with articles by and about you, and while I disagree with several of your views, as I will soon illustrate, you are to me the personification of the balance between idealism and realism that I would like, eventually, to attain.

I have just read your article in the *New York Times Magazine* and there are some things that I would like to say with regard to it. I don't think that the ideal kind of university that Wilson described exists today. If it does exist I can picture it only as an entirely useless entity, useless to the very people it tries to educate, its students. Such an atmosphere of withdrawn study is not possible within the present situation of the world. I picture the "revolt on campus" as a logical result of the state of our nation in the same way that the revolt in the ghettos is the result of our nation's neglect of its people.

23

Both the passive and the active leftists indicate, to some extent, the mood of my entire generation just as the mood of any government can be read in its splinter groups. Though I fully agree with you that these people make up a small minority of the whole, I believe that the forces that give rise to their reactions bear on all the college students all the time; though many, perhaps the majority, of my peers will not heed those forces and will proceed along the path laid out for them, looking neither right nor left, nor inward.

A student who graduates from college this year faces a major doubt in the status of his future. The chance is extremely high that he is going to be drafted. Alternatives like medical school and conscientious objector status are ultimately open to a very few. This confrontation with responsibility is forcing college students to make their decisions about their place in the world, and their nation, early, perhaps too early for a clear analysis of all the facts. We are cornered by a system that we had no part in creating and, more important, we will not have an opportunity, however token, to change it before it works its will on us. At graduation we are immediately faced with an obligation that we have inherited, and we must judge.

This obligation stems directly from the war and bears on the mood of our generation to an incalculable degree. I can remember dimly the aura of noble purpose that surrounded young people during the Kennedy administration. Everywhere they were active in civil rights and programs for bettering the nation. But as the momentum of "the movement" dissipated and the nation girded its loins for war they felt betrayed and reacted with bitterness. This was not the result of a change in the basic makeup of the average nineteen-year-old college student. I think that the same people who participated in the demonstration against Dow Chemical Company here a few months ago would be just as likely to appear at a voter registration drive in Arkansas, at another time and in another situation. The fact that it is not that time and that situation bespeaks a real failure in leadership, not just the standard child's rejections of his parents' world because he must make his own. One of your main objections to the "new left" is that their protest is empty, that they offer no alternatives. I, too, find this regrettable (and am trying to rectify this tendency in myself) but not hard to understand. It has never been the property of the young to provide answers. Rather it has always been their place to reject or support the answers proposed by others. The violence with which this rejection is being voiced today is largely a result of the impotency that we all feel at the hands of "the system." The activists advocate revolution because they do not consider it possible to work from within for a change and the passivists are trying to escape from the monster by ignoring it. The great masses of students, myself included, are just becoming aware of the questions and do not have any answers, but we are all aware that we must have the answers before graduation, the situation requires it.

The fact that Harvard has a prominent place in the

actualities of the world, the fact that it is not only a "think tank" protected from the iniquities of reality is one of the main reasons I came here. Experience is one of the greatest teachers I know of, and though one must sacrifice a certain amount of perspective to involvement, this is a much lesser evil than being sacrificed to someone else's perspective through detachment.

I agree with your view that when one finds fault with a system one must have proposals for the rectification of that fault but how could *I* do this with hope of success? In dictating "life, liberty, and the pursuit of happiness" for all U.S. citizens the Constitution guarantees the freedom of individuality in the face of majority opposition, insofar as that freedom remains individual and does not involve others adversely, does not affect the "common good." Our society has evolved beyond this principle, at least with regard to its young people. We do not constitute a pertinent bloc of voters. We exercise no real power and have little hope of doing so until someone hears us from a position of power and acts on our behalf. Hence "the movement" does not enjoy the position of working for a change but must be content with working for recognition of its validity. The vehemence of our demonstrations reflects the frustration of this situation.

This brings me to the case for civil disobedience where I disagree with you on a vital point. I, too, am against breaking laws with demonstrations to draw attention, simply because I cannot imagine that to be anything but futile. In fact, given the inevitable criterion for

26

the validity of disobedience as measuring the good done to the principle by the harm done to the social order, I feel that in almost every case the law should be respected. In the draft law I find a conspicuous exception. I am not against the draft, though I am emphatically against the way it is being presently employed. I view it as a necessity of the world situation, though an odious one. But I do support those who think that the draft, in conjunction with the war in Vietnam, constitutes a violation of their personal morality. The draft is not a criminal law designed to protect the people from the evils of individuals, nor is it a civil law designed to maintain an economic or political equality. It is a law created solely for providing manpower for enforcing the policies of a government. Much as a tax bill provides money for a war, the draft provides men. In this situation the law is reaching into the personal domain of a man's soul. I think the government can ethically demand that a man offer money for what it considers to be the betterment of society, and time for the same reason. But it is on shaky ground when it asks him to die, and even shakier ground when it asks him to kill. In the end, every individual is responsible to a higher authority than the government and whether it is religious or personal it is sacrosanct. The United States itself held this view in the Nuremberg trials when it found that "following orders" does not excuse one from the consequences of his actions. When one has exhausted all alternatives to fighting and feels definitely that the cause is not just he is, in my opinion, justified in resisting the government's attempts to subvert his morals, though with full knowledge that he is not exempt from the consequences of that resistance.

The crisis of my generation and the reason for the turmoil on the campus is, I feel, that we have to make this essentially moral decision right now, during the years when other equally pressing forces of maturation are confronting us. The actions of the left are, therefore, though not justifiable, understandable and even inevitable. We are turned to bitterness by the impotency of our action. We cannot follow because we are not validly led. We cannot lead because we are not heard. We are unique in the history of this country. The Vietnam "situation" has been so indecisive and agonizing and has gone on so long that we are the first generation in history that is able to view itself as sausages endlessly being fed into a meat grinder. At graduation we face the certainty of some kind of death, moral if not physical, and we must hence do all our living, endure all our agony and ecstasy in four short years. We dwell with the horrible feeling of being a pawn caught in someone else's chess game. Is it any wonder that we are disenchanted with the society that could give rise to this situation? Is it any wonder that we "do not go gentle into that good night"?

> Respectfully,
> DAVID C. KING
> Harvard '71

New York, N.Y., January 21, 1968

Dear Mr. Kennan:

I am currently a senior at Columbia University who has long been one of your admirers. My interest and studies of Soviet affairs and my intention to pursue a career of research into Soviet politics have strengthened this admiration and added to it an ideology. I was both impressed and depressed by your recent article on radical student politics that appeared in the *New York Times Magazine*. I have agreed in the past, and even now in the present, tend emotionally to agree with your ideals. But as a responsible citizen, devoted to America, I have found it increasingly difficult to remain detached in my academic cloisters. And as a draft-eligible young man, a student whose academic pursuits are clouded by the ever-present fear of losing my life in those Vietnam jungles, I find it morally impossible to live with myself without actively opposing the war and the conditions that foster it and are fostered by it. I should not fear giving up my life for my country when I would feel that I were truly fighting for my country. I and my fellow students are unwilling to sacrifice what our parents have given us in material comfort and moral training, and what our country has given us in opportunity and freedom to use that opportunity for a cause which, to our eyes, is both politically and morally wrong. Nor are we so entranced by the rectitude and certainty of our cause that we do not question, do not doubt. But one cannot

29

hesitate or have mixed feelings if he is to fight, to kill, to destroy.

I hope that you can feel something of the urgency I am experiencing and sympathize with the desperate political activities on the campus.

Respectfully yours,
ARTHUR R. BREGMAN
Columbia '68

Princeton, N.J., January 21, 1968

Dear Mr. Kennan:

I am a graduate student here at the University and, after reading your article in today's *Times Magazine,* I thought I would like to share some of my reactions with you.

Though I am neither a political activist nor a hippie — and, though I find myself repelled by the characteristic practices of both these groups — I find myself confronting the same world that they confront and, from both observation and introspection, I think I have come to some understanding of the reactions of a sensitive person facing such a world.

I believe that Ortega y Gasset was quite correct when he said, almost forty years ago, that the Western world had once again entered a period of "historical crisis," a time of disorientation and extremism. He compared the present to the previous crises of the West, those of the Hellenistic world and of the later Middle

Ages and paid special attention to the discussion of the latter by Johan Huizinga in his *Waning of the Middle Ages.*

I highly recommend this book to anyone who is seeking a better understanding of my generation and the society in which it has come to maturity. Huizinga describes a world characterized by violence, by pessimism, by a breakdown of formerly held concepts of order (aggravated by, among other things, the schism in the Church and the belief that nobody could enter Heaven while it lasted). Men reacted by forming mystic cults, by producing art and literature that, as in [the] case of chivalric literature, sentimentalized a vestige of the older order and invested it with a full vocabulary of symbolism so full and so ornate that, finally, there were symbols for everything one could say; and by engaging in "the most horrible crimes and the most extravagant acts of saintliness."

Ortega observed that men in a period of historical crisis are desperately looking for something in which they can believe. Consequently they will characteristically go from one manifestation of extremism to another but will be unable to find anything in which they are genuinely happy. Ortega would have questioned Robert Kennedy's implication that there was a qualitative change involved when young people went from S.D.S. to L.S.D. Such people were drawn to the one for the same reason that they were drawn to the other and will, most likely, find satisfaction in neither.

Hippies and political extremists would have been as

out of place in the monasteries of the High Middle Ages as they would have been in Wilson's Princeton. I find the hippies akin to the love cultists, the flagellants and others out of Huizinga's world. In a period in which the world is in order, we do not have mass cultural movements of this sort and one can just as well say that in Wilson's day these people would have been at school or at their jobs or in any other normal place.

Another factor common to both the post-Medieval and, if you will, post-Modern worlds seems to be a destruction of the faith in order combined with a destruction of the old form and order on all sides. Huizinga's world had had its outlook conditioned by the Black Death, bloody wars, the schism in the Church, etc. We have had two world wars, the Nazi death camps, the development of highly efficient atomic and hydrogen bombs and related phenomena to deal with. Many have had their faith in a world order shaken by such things, as is rather obvious. Wilson's world is, unfortunately, dead.

We have a technology that has been busily liberating man from his sense of doing meaningful work and a society so vast and technologized that many feel they will be deprived of all individuality unless they offer total resistance. Moreover, everything about us stresses instantaneousness of gratification of wants. We can travel anywhere in a matter of hours or days. We can communicate instantly, get entertained instantly, etc. And the nightmare world of the 21st Century will just be more of the same! Is it any wonder that young people living in this climate want instant spiritual fulfillment, instant physical gratification, instant change in the political and social system? Not only do these people not have the capacity, borne of their environment, for hard work towards rational goals but they do not even have the patience for the long, hard meditation of the Asian mystic and they take L.S.D. as a seeming shortcut.

Contempt for the law by some of these people is a consequence of ways in which the law has made itself contemptible. Can people who see the law protecting slumlords (by fixing ridiculously small fines for violations), protecting Southern whites whose murder victims happen to be Negroes, allowing tax loopholes for the rich, etc., be expected to conclude that law is something superhuman and sacred instead of the expression of the will of those who have influence?

When young people read study after study showing how America's social classes are becoming more, not less, clearly distinguishable and how important lineage and wealth are in determining who shall be who in the various hierarchies (I refer, for example, to Vance Packard's *The Status Seekers*) and they see how social problems just do not seem to get solved, is it any wonder that they conclude that a revolution would offer a far greater opportunity for them to actualize their ideals (if they are still sufficiently influenced by Wilson's world to have ideals and not among those whose "ideals" are merely a manifestation of extremism and not something deeply held in and of themselves) than would the give and take — mainly take — of dealing with the *status quo*. After all, as the world gets bigger and fuller, it becomes impossible to be heard. You have to get into the mass media and violence is one sure way to do it.

I agree with you that one of the most terrible results of youthful extremism has been the alienation of parents and children. I would suggest that there might be a cause of the break of the great "golden chain of affection" that has not received much mention. I refer to the nuclear American family structure. Many of these young people's parents identified coming of age with the severing of ties with *their* parents, who were no longer "necessary." Widespread geographic mobility has further weakened the ties to the old people. Many of the young people know that their parents regard their grandparents as a financial liability and shut them out of their lives. (2500 years ago, Confucius denounced those who make sure their parents are fed and think they are being filial sons. After all, he said, they would do as much for their horses.) Perhaps the golden chain has been severed before you come to the youngest link.

Coincidentally, your article appeared in the same issue as a feature about Rumania, in which the author mentioned the pervasive cynicism one encounters there and which has been a result of centuries of being pushed around by forces beyond the people's control. I would contend that many of my peers feel themselves at the mercy of those forces which they know they cannot control. After all, is not one of our major industries, advertising, based on the idea that people have to be manipulated into buying things they do not need? The draft is a source of anxiety to many and there *is* something

Kafkaesque about its whole manner of operation.

Our culture tries to make children into adults as quickly as possible, it seems. Whether it be adult-type clothing, preparation for college, ridiculously premature dating, or whatever, kids are given reason to think of themselves as adults earlier than ever. When they encounter such things as parietal rules and drinking laws, they rebel against not being treated like adults. Some, indeed, seem to feel that they are being singled out for discrimination in a society in which formerly revered moral standards are being shot down right and left. This is another factor that adds to their cynicism. And the closer cynicism comes to being a general attitude, instead of merely being directed against some particular, the more difficult it becomes to do purposeful work. One tends to become cynical about the goal.

A malaise that I have encountered among graduate students (the leadership corps of many student upheavals) is also worth mentioning. A university in our society is not the calm place that Wilson sought. When, for example, the experiment is not succeeding, it is not uncommon for the student to feel that he is not going anywhere and become discouraged and feel that he has been wasting his energy. To such a student, it is a great relief to be able to do something "meaningful," like take part in a demonstration. Perhaps some also look to drugs for a release from the sense of purposelessness. It was all right for a Medieval monk to spend his days copying illuminated manuscripts. He was not pressed for time and his future, culminating in entrance to

Heaven, was secure. But the graduate student, in his moments of uncertainty, knows that he will have to support a family someday and will have his employment chances impaired if he lacks the degree. In a Calvinist society, the pressure to achieve was bad enough but it did not have to coexist with a hedonism that stresses immediacy and a technology that renders the future problematical.

I trust you do not carry to extremes your statement that the "decisive seat of evil in this world is . . . in the weakness and imperfection of the human soul itself." I hope you are not denying that some men are a good deal more evil than others and are not proposing quietism as an alternative to the destruction of evil institutions. I prefer not to get into a discussion of the theology of original sin or lack of same but I would suggest that a person born and raised in a society that sanctions slavery or racial discrimination will be a good deal more evil to members of the out-group than someone born in a place where the institutions do not conflict with the idea of total equality. Ultimately, you are probably correct, but to what extent is this belief to affect action for social betterment?

Ortega y Gasset saw the historical crisis of the post-Medieval world as finally ending with the emergence of modern rationalism, of Cartesian man. He suggested that the present period would ultimately give way to some new equilibrium. The way things are going, though, I find it difficult to detect any improvement in the essential quality of life in the foreseeable future. (Probably many who turn to drugs and/or political ex-

36

tremism also feel this way.) My great hope is that some people will find fulfillment by refusing to have the robots do everything for them and rediscovering artisan skills and the art of tilling the soil without the interference of machinery. But, alas, maybe this Tolstoyan Romanticism is just another form of extremism.

I hope you have found this letter interesting. I am privileged to have an opportunity to communicate my thoughts to a person of your stature.

Yours truly,
MICHAEL L. TICKTIN
Graduate Student
Princeton University

New Haven, Conn., January 23, 1968

To the Editor:

Although I tend to agree with the conclusion Mr. Kennan reaches in his article of January 21, that neither the militants nor the hippies of today's youth are accomplishing their avowed purposes and that this failure is in large part due to the failure of their methods to fit the criteria established by the ideals, nevertheless I cannot accept his theory that the cause of these mistakes lies in the original unjustified venture by the students into the realm of active interest in their society.

More than just the militant left wing of today's campuses must be upset by Mr. Kennan's theory that the process of education and learning implicitly denies the right of the student to engage himself in facing the problems he sees around him. In fact what makes today's campuses exciting is the awareness among a majority of the students that the fact of education creates a responsibility to the community to use the abilities they are developing. Of growing concern in education today is the necessity of establishing this relationship between thought and action.

In contradiction to this element of education, Mr. Kennan's theory would seem to deny the value of such programs as Harvard's Phillips Brooks House or Yale's Grant Foundation or a host of other programs at campuses across the country that are designed to give students a chance to act on their community's problems. The students working in these programs are not necessarily militants or hippies.

Every individual must feel frustrated by the seeming impossibility of ever leaving his mark on the huge bulwark of our society. It is not surprising, therefore, that some in my generation resort to faster and more dramatic means to leave their dent or that others seek to escape from the problem altogether. But to condemn today's students, wholesale, because they are ready to commit themselves in a fight against the evils they see and because the restlessness inside them forces them to act now instead of waiting for some great moment in their future when they suddenly stop learning and are ready to act, is to condemn the element in my generation that is most exciting and which will eventually show itself as the key to our strength.

Sincerely,
HUGH AUCHINCLOSS, JR.
Yale '71

Brooklyn, N.Y., January 31, 1968

To the Editor:

George Kennan's comments about "Rebels Without a Program" make a great deal of sense to one who has lived since 1958 through the very beginnings of the hippie and New Left movements at Berkeley. However, his comments lack a certain perspective which very few members of the "over-30 generation" possess.

For the past year-and-a-half, I have lived and worked in the Bedford-Stuyvesant community of Brooklyn, second largest "ghetto" area in the nation, as an anti-poverty worker. I have seen what American society does to those who are black and to those who are poor.

Eight years at Berkeley among the New Left and the hippies left me with liberal Democratic views resembling those of Kennan — but Bedford-Stuyvesant has turned me into a revolutionary. Supposedly, one grows more conservative as one grows older, but the older many youth of my generation get, the more they see of American society, the more radical they become.

The police in Bedford-Stuyvesant are like a colonial

army of occupation, the schools like prisons, the welfare department merely another variation of the slavemaster system in which husband and wife are separated and the husband humiliated.

Kennan of all people should know that there have been numerous programs for helping people in poor communities but these programs are either ill-conceived; or if well-conceived are unsuccessful because of sabotage by local politicians, educational bureaucrats or others; or finally if successful, are kept small and token.

For example, Bedford-Stuyvesant, second largest black community in the country, does not have an Upward Bound — the highly successful War on Poverty program in which 80% of its non-college-bound poor youth go on to higher education. Bedford-Stuyvesant has no Upward Bound because two years ago, none of the ten colleges in Brooklyn cared enough about the community to even bother applying. Last year when two colleges were urged into applying, no money was available because Congress has consistently refused to increase this highly successful program to meet the desperate needs of low income youth for special higher education programs.

There are many, many people who are working hard on concrete programs in Bedford-Stuyvesant and elsewhere but most of these efforts are hamstrung by the callous, racist and dehumanizing character of American society. Things do change in America, but slowly, and while they change so slowly, thousands of precious, beautiful children in poor communities are crippled and destroyed by the American jungle which surrounds them.

Many of Kennan's criticisms of the hippies and New Left have also been made repeatedly by people like myself, offspring of the "Establishment" but alienated from the status quo. I agree with his criticisms but I can add only that any man who is not angry and not militant about changing America either does not know or does not care about the brutality perpetrated every day upon the streets of America under the cloak of "freedom" and "democracy."

Faithfully yours,
DAVID LEE
University of California '66

New York, N.Y., January 21, 1968

To the Editor:

Mr. George Kennan's praise of the separation of theory from practice represents succinctly, though insidiously, a good deal of what is making many of us angry. I am not referring to the insinuations of infantilism and worse ("eyes glazed with anger . . . dimmed by artificial abuse of the psychic structure") but to what I take to be the substance of his argument — that "a certain remoteness from the contemporary scene . . . a certain voluntary withdrawal and renunciation of participation in contemporary life" is necessary for learning to take place, so that students should avoid political activity until their education is over (whatever that means).

Now it is a truism that students should study, but the implication that studying excludes political activity is insidious. Isn't it arbitrary, after all, to draw the line at graduation? And what leads Mr. Kennan to the view that learning is so very separate from doing?

Contrary to what Mr. Kennan suggests, many of us in the so-called New Left — when not busy "ranting and raving" — have been concerned precisely with the character of our education and of our universities. That "the perfect site of learning" Mr. Kennan extols is not just a cop out but an impossibility has become painfully clear to us. With universities becoming increasingly service stations for military and corporate interests, it is likely that retreat even into the most "academic" disciplines is itself, consciously or not, interest-laden and even beneficial to an oppressive status quo. We have learned that "the end of ideology" and the image of a value-free university are myths invoked to sanction quite interest-laden activities — like military research and recruiting, and "channeling" into the socio-economic elite. It is particularly incongruous that Mr. Kennan, whom even Walter Lippmann credits as a major ideologist of the Cold War, should argue for value-free universities.

Now of course we do have a great deal to learn, and it is no secret, especially to Mr. Kennan, that revolutionary practice requires revolutionary theory. But it is a commonplace that we learn, at least in part, by doing. Thus in being "charged and dragged about by police," many of us have learned more about America than we could in years of quiet study in libraries.

42

Mr. Kennan chides us for not having alternative programs. This is puzzling in that, say, the program of immediate withdrawal of American troops from Vietnam is certainly clearer and very probably more rational than anything "responsible" critics like Mr. Kennan or their counterparts in the Departments of State and Defense have suggested. Of course public policy is "complex" and the left does lack well worked out alternatives, though not to the extent that Mr. Kennan insinuates. But is the blame here ours, or does it lie with those to whom we might look for wisdom if only they would not so zealously and self-servingly embrace the mythology of the "perfect place of learning"?

Throughout his article, Mr. Kennan repeatedly charges us with naïveté and adolescent idealism, for which he pities us. He concedes that the Vietnam War or "individual situations . . . such as the conditions of the Negroes in our great cities" might be thought intolerable. But he rejects our fervor. Yet in a world where the American military and the interests it serves are regarded as the main enemy by the people of three continents, and where in defense of these interests the American government is waging a genocidal war against the people of Vietnam, doesn't it become grotesque to patronize the outrage of those who dissent from American policy fervently? One wonders whether Mr. Kennan is not so sophisticated and "realistic" as to merit pity himself!

Finally, we are blamed for not realizing that "weakness and imperfection . . . lie in the human soul" and not in political and social institutions. Without pretending to Mr. Kennan's authority in these matters, I suggest it is reasonable to hold that institutions, if not perfectible, are at least improvable to a point where war and poverty, exploitation and racism, can disappear. Once this is granted it should not require too much withdrawn reflection in academic retreats to make the necessary intellectual connections . . .

ANDREW LEVINE
Columbia University Students
for a Democratic Society (SDS)

Cambridge, Mass., February 11, 1968

To the Editor:

Many thanks to George Kennan for his perceptive analysis of student "Rebels Without a Program" (Jan. 21). As might be expected, however, your letters column indicates it has given young radicals small pause for introspection. One should never have hoped, of course, that reason would convince them that their glorious revolutionary ideals might not be right, or that they just might not be consistent with the atmosphere of learning that a university presumably has. Nonetheless, it was refreshing to find that somewhere, someone still thinks that scholarship is the academic ideal; for S.D.S.'ers evidently do not.

S.D.S. ("Students for a Democratic Society," as they style themselves) is the symbol of campus radical-

44

ism, and no doubt its leaders feel smugly self-satisfied in this notoriety: they have worked hard enough to attain it. They have organized petitions, demonstrations, sit-ins, lock-ins, and progressively more violent means to protest causes as diverse as the coming of an official of Dow Chemical Co. (proscribed because it makes napalm for the war) and a proposed increase in Boston subway fares (damnable because it would only further enrich fat capitalists). And if petitions or demonstrations — both of which are perfectly legitimate; I have no objection to these, as long as they do not disrupt the peace — do not make Lyndon Johnson change his war policy, nor Dow change its business, then, like little children not getting the attention they feel their actions deserve, they must use "more forceful" means in order to be heard. That is why they locked a Dow representative in a Harvard building for six hours, excusing their action on grounds of "freedom of speech."

Curiously enough, S.D.S. would ban Marine and C.I.A. on-campus recruiting. Its reasoning is perfectly sound. The U.S. government (read Lyndon Johnson) is suppressing freedom around the world, and therefore has no right to enjoy the freedom it guarantees to S.D.S. Who has decided that the United States is suppressing freedom, and therefore should not be accorded it? S.D.S., of course. . . . All of which is in the best Mao-ist tradition of revolution.

I do not mean to imply that S.D.S. members are evil, or totalitarian, or impossible to get along with; indeed, some of my best friends are S.D.S.'ers. I do think, though, that in playing at revolution, secure in their ivory tower, they have forgotten the purpose of university education. They are carried away by all the passions of youth, yet pretend to be responsible. It is a peculiar trait of the S.D.S. member to be perfectly pleasant, even rational, until matters concerning public policy become the theme of conversation; then the eyes turn fiery and he becomes livid, shouting his Truth and his Righteousness at one sitting in the same room. A very peculiar trait indeed.

I know S.D.S.'ers at both Princeton and Harvard; true, I cannot judge if they are "far more knowledgeable and sophisticated, far less imprisoned by myth and ideology, than the average undergraduate," as Professor Duberman claims; but nor am I imprisoned by their vague but "angry" ideology that damns the society that has pampered them. There are a lot of injustices in the present system, but it is the Eugene McCarthys, the John Lindsays, and perhaps most of all the Lyndon Johnsons (anathema!) who will correct them — certainly not the students rioting at Whitehall, screaming tired Marxist slogans, or dreaming up revolutions.

Sincerely,
JEFFREY LAURENTI
Harvard '71

To the Editor:

George Kennan, in his article "Rebels Without a Program," chastises the student Left for failing to create a systematic political ideology capable of serving as a basis for constructive change. It seems to me that Mr. Kennan's generation, and not the student protesters, must answer for the ideological bankruptcy with which America faces crises in race relations and in Viet Nam. Mr. Kennan, with all his experience and scholarly discipline, has himself failed to offer relevant new ideas, so how can he expect inexperienced and undisciplined young people to do any better? Faced with a crying demand for intellectual leadership in a desperate new situation, Kennan responds by telling us that we must respect our elders and restrain our emotions. All well and good, but this really isn't much help.

Hans Schmidt
Graduate Student
Rutgers University

Newburgh, N.Y., January 27, 1968

To the Editor:

As a graduate student of political science and an admirer of George Kennan, I was disappointed and dismayed by his article "Rebels Without a Program." The very qualities I had admired in Mr. Kennan — his perception and his analytical ability — were sorely lacking.

Mr. Kennan's characterization of the student activist demonstrators as "screaming, throwing stones, breaking windows, overturning cars, being beaten or dragged about by police" shows that he has relied for his information largely on the mass media, and particularly on television, which naturally focus on violent demonstrations and on the violent incidents in peaceful demonstrations. Such a characterization is untrue and unfair, for it smears the concerned, active majority with the failings of a fringe minority. Surely Mr. Kennan himself has, at some time, taken part in a public event which was distorted by the mass media.

Further, Mr. Kennan seems to assume that this generation of students is somehow strikingly different from any other in its lack of concentrated effort on its studies. How many students in Mr. Kennan's university days were immersed in their books while their fellows were out on the football field "screaming" "Bull Dog"? The assumption that the student who goes on a demonstration has less time to study than the student who is active in sports or in social events is patently false. (One might add that it is difficult for some students to remain detached when their studies may be interrupted by the draft.)

One could, however, excuse the faulty perceptions if Mr. Kennan's analysis of the present situation were less superficial. The active student (and the hippy) are two examples of what social scientists call the alienated individual. In the past decade, much scholarly work has been done about alienations. Yet Mr. Kennan shows no acquaintance with this literature in his discussion.

Nor does he seek the reasons behind the phenomena he deplores. I submit that he would have drawn a less superficial and more pessimistic picture had he dug a little deeper. To take but a few examples:

Why does the active student take to the streets instead of discussing these affairs "with knowledge and without passion"? One answer is that the energy expended on the street could well be applied in the classroom if more social science departments offered courses about race relations, urban problems, and Vietnam. Many students find that their university experience is divorced from reality and therefore reject the scholastic tradition which, as Mr. Kennan says, has so much to offer.

Why do these demonstrators cry out "virtually meaningless slogans"? Why is there this "extraordinary degree of certainty . . . of one's own rectitude . . . certainty as to the iniquity of those who disagree"? One can only urge Mr. Kennan to turn to the front page of his favorite newspaper and read the words our leaders use in talking about the ponderous problems with which youth is concerned. "Meaningless slogans" and "certainty as to the iniquity of those who disagree" are not the private domain of the young. Are such slogans as "communist aggression" and "crime in the streets" any more meaningful than "freedom now" or "end the war"? Is not "nervous nellies" an example of "certainty as to the iniquity . . ."? Such verbiage is the common political currency of the day. The "irresponsible" youth are but copying the style of their "responsible" leaders.

Finally, Mr. Kennan is quite correctly alarmed by what he calls "a disconcerting resemblance to the phenomena we have witnessed within our own time in the origins of totalitarianism in other countries." As an historian, however, he must be aware that no historian blames the Nazi and Fascist takeovers of democratic systems on what Secretary of State Dean Rusk calls "storm trooper tactics." What Mr. Kennan and Mr. Rusk remark is a resemblance of symptoms, not of causes. To understand the causes of these types of situations, they may be advised to look at the lack of effective, attractive, imaginative political leadership necessary to solve the pressing problems of the day and to channel the enthusiasm and hope of youth into constructive activities.

One must therefore disagree with Mr. Kennan's conclusion that "we have no choice but to rally to the defense of a public authority with which we may not be in agreement but which is the only one we've got . . ." This is no more constructive than the activities of the students. Rather, one might hope that people like Mr. Kennan, who have the wisdom and the discipline of scholarship, would come forth and join forces with the active students, bringing them the wisdom, the dispassion, the constructive program and the leadership which they so desperately need.

MARGARET KENT BROOKS
Graduate Student
Columbia University

Cambridge, Mass., January 24, 1968

To the Editor:

As one of the "angry ones," I find that I must register my protest against George Kennan's article. I wish to concern myself with the issue of Vietnam since almost all student protest centers around this problem.

Professor Kennan brings up the old line about no alternative program being offered by the left. I suggest that anyone who still believes this charge take a look at the New York Times editorial that appeared the same day as the article — "Alternatives in Vietnam."

He also presents the ideal of a scholar's disciplined study, pointing out that the issues of the day are so complex that one could easily devote years of detached study to them before presenting one's views. I cannot express how terribly evil I feel this view is. How long did it take the Nazis to murder six million Jews? Does anyone doubt that the United States has the technological capability to destroy the entire population of Vietnam within a week if our government really wanted to? The issues of the day are so important that one cannot, in good conscience, wait years before attempting to make the Administration listen to one's views.

Professor Kennan also feels that the vigor of the protest is incompatible with successful study of the problems. I should like to point out that when those in control are of the opposite view, it is necessary to make one's protest strong in order to get the other side to listen. Furthermore, the resistance of the anti-war peo-

51

ple to listen to other points of view is probably not nearly as strong as the resistance of the Administration, which realizes that if it listens, it will have to explain to the American people why it has sent 50,000 American soldiers to die in Vietnam.

There is also the question of just how detached a student can be when the government gives him just four years of study before sending him off to participate in the destruction of Vietnam.

DAVID CANE
M.I.T. '69

Princeton, N.J.

To the Editor:

I find it necessary to reply to Mr. Kennan's article ("Rebels Without a Program," Jan. 21) because, as I feared, a growing number of adults are using it as a convenient weapon with which they can attack student activities. I would like to make three major points concerning Mr. Kennan's article.

First of all, Mr. Kennan states that students often act compulsively and without collecting sufficient information. Let me just say that a college student has not yet made his peace with society. He is willing to take actions he would not be willing to take later in life when he has gained more knowledge through academic pursuits and added experience. Once he starts a job, he finds

52

he has too much of a stake in society to risk protesting against it.

Secondly, even though student actions are often irrational and compulsive, I feel that they are valuable to society. In a free society like ours, there should be no sacred cows (Moo to you, Mr. Hoover). The often "hyper-Socratic" methods of campus activists act as a valuable cleansing agent for society. I believe it was Justice Holmes who said that the mark of a civilized man is the ability to question one's most cherished beliefs. A good example of what I mean happened at Princeton. Several students sat in at the IDA (Institute for Defense Analyses) to protest the University's alleged tie with the organization. The students' action was compulsive and somewhat uninformed. Yet as it turned out, there were, *at least*, many aspects of the IDA–Princeton relationship that needed questioning. A committee has been appointed to investigate the matter. Here was a clear-cut case of compulsive student action raising an important issue that, left to the "knowledgeable" adult world, would have never been raised.

Thirdly, Mr. Kennan calls for the "Campus Left" to develop some unified program. This is impossible since "Campus Left" is only a euphemism for a series of *ad hoc* reactions by a myriad of students protesting a myriad of problems at a myriad of different schools and locales. Due to the different nature of the problems on the different campuses, and due to a turnover that would bar any continuity, I feel there never can be a monolithic entity called the "Campus Left." After all, we don't expect a program from the "Adult Right" either. Both groups are merely chimerical inventions.

Lastly I would like to say that I have met and deeply admire Mr. Kennan. I think that his article was especially unfortunate because I know that he has a great deal more sympathy for student activities than do those who use his article in a "Now George has come over" fashion.

DAVID GOULD
Princeton '68

Norwich, Vt., January 21, 1968

To the Editor:

As a member of the student Left, I must take exception to many of George Kennan's criticisms in his "Rebels Without a Program." First, I do not know where Mr. Kennan got the idea that the student Left is "violent." For the most part, our anti-war activities have followed the same principles of non-violence which, until recently, were the hallmark of the civil rights movement. After all, where did we learn our tactics? Violence, where it has occurred, has been on the part of the police authorities.

As to the question of when civil disobedience is justified in a democratic society, one must ask if this is the right question to ask at all. In any society, democratic or otherwise, when one sees injustice, one must resist. Nor should he get "hung-up" in an abstract debate over the

54

issue of civil disobedience violating someone's rights or principles. If I see a woman being murdered on the street, I do not stop to ask if I will be violating her attacker's rights or abstract democratic principles before taking some kind of action. In the light of what is being done in Vietnam today, therefore, the answer to the question of when civil disobedience is justified becomes very simple: Now!

Contrary to Mr. Kennan's belief, the student Left does have some idea of the type of society we would like to see in this country. It is a society established on the principle of people controlling their own destinies and those institutions which govern their lives. The student Left has also attempted to determine what must be done to create such a society, and we have found that it will take much more than constitutional amendments or simple political reform. It will take nothing less than the radical transformation of the economic, social, and political structure of this society. If Mr. Kennan can come up with a simpler solution, we will be only too glad to listen to it.

But may I suggest that he is not likely to find such a solution by confining himself to the ivory tower of academia. The student Left grew out of nothing less than a protest against the irrelevance of the academic community to what is going on in the world. This irrelevancy is not at all strange. After all, it is the nature of the academic's work to order the world so that he may explain it. History has shown that at times when the world defies ordering, in times of violent change (the Russian and French Revolutions, for example), the academic community becomes irrelevant. All it can do is to wait for some stability to return to the world and then attempt to explain what has occurred during the period of change. The world today, and particularly the United States, is in such a state of violent change, and it is not surprising that those who seem best able to explain it are those most involved in the whole process of change. We may not be "students" by Mr. Kennan's definition of the term, but at least we are attempting to be relevant to the forces of change in the world today.

Yours for peace,
LEE T. BRIDGES
Dartmouth '68

Cambridge, Mass., January 21, 1968

To the Editor:

I was surprised that George Kennan, a scholar with such respect for fact, could have so completely missed the point in his article "Rebels Without a Program." He writes that when young people "attempt to alter the workings of the system by means of violence or civil disobedience, this . . . can have only one of two implications." Either they believe that our democracy has ceased to be representative, or they do not believe in democracy at all.

I would say there is a third implication in this surge

of "illegal" protest. It is this: the Administration has not faced up to a responsibility at least as integral to democracy as respect for law and order, the responsibility to engage its critics in honest debate. We want not slogans, but a justification of American policy based on fact. We of the opposition happen to feel that no such factual justification is possible; that our intervention and eventual creation of a civil war in Vietnam was against international law, our own national interest, and the larger interests of self-determination and stability in Asia. But this does not justify the Administration's refusal to grapple with the content (not the methods) of the opposition, in Senate hearings or on the campus. Senator Fulbright put this well when he said (The New York Times, December 9, 1967): "Dissenters do not dissent for the mere pleasure of hearing themselves orate, or of being seen on television, or of enjoying the democratic right of free speech. They dissent because they wish to have an impact on events," in a word, to be taken seriously. But "the hearings held before the Foreign Relations Committee have demonstrated — thus far — that the Administration is as unreceptive to the views of Senators, experienced diplomats and eminent scholars as it is to the views of the young firebrands of the New Left . . . In making the distinction between orderly dissent, of which it professes to approve, and disorderly dissent, of which we all disapprove, the Administration seems unable to understand that it is the futility of the one that has given rise to the other."

Until the Administration faces up to its obligation, it

should not censure citizens for their exasperation and, in certain cases, even a breach of the social contract.

Sincerely,
CARYL GEPPERT
Graduate Student
Harvard University

Toronto, Canada

To the Editor:

Re George Kennan's article on the campus left:

The reason we criticize without offering alternative is understandable: we know enough to know what we don't want, but not enough to know what should be done about it. We ask the older generation to explain why things are the way they are (which they don't sometimes — witness the credibility gap), help us to find the alternatives, show us the tools to build the alternative (other than our present method, protest, what can we do?) and lastly work with us.

CHALMERS HARDENBERGH
University of Toronto

Rochester, N.Y., January 29, 1968

To the Editor:

Having remained a quiescent undergraduate firmly believing the gospel of the academic spirit, I feel particularly qualified to respond to Mr. Kennan's remarks. My eyes have not been dimmed "by the artificial abuse of the psychic structure" — rather my mind and sensibilities have been assaulted and abused by the world of Huntley-Brinkley. In the age of mass media, it takes a certain talent to avoid the constant barrage of news of the passing world. It requires a willed and cultivated deafness to withdraw from the contemporary world, and it requires a callous inhumanity not to be absorbed with the absurdity of the contemporary scene.

Furthermore, it take tragically little knowledge to perceive the mindlessness that pervades our social scene. Does it require any technical skill to recognize the gross inadequacies and injustices of this society? In the name of reason, imperialism abroad and repression at home continue to escalate. Calm administrators explain away death and destruction. In short, rational process has given way to obstinate rationalization; thinking has been replaced by belligerent justification.

Cloaked in the armor of law, order, reason and God, we engage in world-wide repression, all the while ignoring the pressing demands of our own society. Does it take years of study to realize the demands of people to will their own destiny? Does it require a solid background in economic theory to understand that black Americans refuse to live as second-class citizens?

American youth asks for a change in the way this society thinks. Priorities simply must be changed. It does not require knowledge to shift the social perspective. Organized programs can come later — first people must be convinced of the absolute necessity of a new approach to American society. Calm reflection and technical programs will be important when we all are of the conviction that internal problems deserve top priority.

For the academic to withdraw to the solitary remoteness of the study is simply repugnant. We all share in the crime of complacency. To willfully blind oneself to the demands of the temporal world in this era of great social turbulence is nothing but immoral. To calmly speak the language of sterile rationality while all about us people die absurdly is criminal. It is time for those who place their faith in the order of the rational mind to heed the call of the heart: unnecessary slaughter and destruction are not worth the price this society may have to pay. I, for one, am very tired of the plea for further knowledge and study. It takes precious little knowledge to see where the greatest demands upon this society are located. What is required at this time is not a careful program of reform — what is required is the sense of the urgent need for any reform. This sense of urgency will not be fostered on the campus; unfortunately, it must be dramatized in picket lines and on the streets.

ALAN FINDER
Rochester '69

To the Editor:

I don't propose to speak for everyone of my age, but I am not untypical of many. I am a senior at Yale University. My father is a judge and I come from a moderate middle middle-class home in California with family roots firmly buried in the Midwest and in the South. I have never sat-in. I have not dropped out. I am, however, a radical by Mr. Kennan's definition. Although I have not burned my draft card, I fully expect to spend five years of my life in federal prison for refusing to go to the war in Vietnam.

I have decided to act in this manner for many reasons. In sum, though, I have decided that American democracy can collapse and is presently near collapse and that I cannot personally consent to the demands which the present policies of failure would impose upon me. I am saying many things by saying this, and it seems important that these things be explained.

I am saying, first, that I think that the American democratic institution is not a fool-proof one. I am not saying that I would destroy it. Almost every criticism I would offer of the present situation is a criticism of an institution which has permitted certain people to gain power and to wield power in such a reckless fashion as to jeopardize the existence of the entire institution which bestowed that power upon them. To say this is not to say I believe in some other system than democracy. I've never found any other system which would as a betting

61

proposition provide better returns. I might revamp this democracy a bit. I might get rid of the seniority system in Congress and get rid of it quick. I might institute greater congressional power in the domain of foreign affairs. I might get rid of the electoral college. I might break the stranglehold of the political establishment on party nomination procedure. I might make a whole host of ameliorating suggestions. But I would not propose a frontal assault on democracy nor even the 1968 American brand — because I'm not at all certain that my proposals would offer any certain solution to the present dilemma or to similar dilemmas in the future. By and large I'm satisfied with American democracy as an institution — because I don't believe in institutional perfection and I realize that every improvement in one element of any system generally weakens another someplace else.

But to say that I acquiesce to the form is not to say that I accept its content. Any system regardless of its political hue is no better nor worse than those people who run it. I do not believe in American democracy really. I merely accept it. I believe in wise, intelligent, and knowing men. I believe in government by the ablest. I believe in a better life by better minds. American democracy has been able to provide this through the years, and to that extent I wish to congratulate American democracy on its good fortune. But there's nothing inherent in American democracy which perpetuates government by the best minds. In fact there's a frightening number of forces in the system working in just the contrary direction. And today it seems to me luck is not with us, for those forces are prevailing. Government is not the instrument of enlightened statesmen, but the plaything of ignorant and psychologically torn men. There are few good men in government. And those who are good are relatively without power. This is to say, then, that I'm willing to posit that a single-party authoritarian state can meet the demands of a society every bit as capably as American democracy has met the demands of its society, if its leaders are able and wise. As long as the best men rule, I'd say the product would be more or less benign. In all cases the criterion which rides always above the nature of the institutional structure itself is the quality of the men within it.

Thus my present concern for America lies not really with its institutions and so it is relatively unimportant what I would suggest in the form of amendments unless those amendments do contribute to the rise of talent to the top. Most of the amendments I suggest are designed to facilitate this. But I view them as relatively insignificant and Mr. Kennan's demand that I enunciate them as gratuitous. My present concern lies with the men who man the present institution. My despair has grown out of my fear of the present and not out of my pessimism over the far-off future of America and her institutional continuity.

This despair is perhaps more deep-seated than one might think. Normally one could rectify the chronic deficiency of good minds in government by campaigning for the election of better minds. But today in 1968 the answer to this dilemma is not so simple.

First, America is ignorant of the world in which she lives. She misunderstands the forces which have awakened two-thirds of the world and sent it into a generation of revolution. She over-simplifies and then exaggerates defensively when these over-simplifications are challenged. Not merely her leaders do this, her grass-roots democratic man does it. It is not only that the men who man the political institution are ignorant but that they are a reflection of the populace which is ignorant (and which they unwittingly maintain in ignorance, it must be added). The election process is predicated upon the intelligence and awareness of the electorate. The college generation has little faith in either when the American people are concerned, at least today in 1968. Thus we have little hope for amelioration through the election process.

Secondly, even should the electorate be knowledgeable, an alternative which conforms to the realization of that knowledge must be offered. It is almost impossible that such an alternative will be offered, given our party politics.

But, thirdly, and so much more significantly, there must be time for change and there is no time. There must be time for education of the electorate, there must be time for democratic process, and there must be time for institutional evolution. And today, Mr. Kennan, there is no time. The urgency of the problem is incalculable. An entire nation of people might be obliterated from the face of the earth or even worse utterly demoralized by the time an election which will promise them relief rolls around. The ghettos of America might spew out into every nook and cranny of the land before the comprehensive assault is made on racism and poverty which new personnel in government might offer. Thousands and thousands of our best youths might go to jail as a horrible sacrifice to ignorance because they had nor voice nor vote, undeniably depriving the nation of many of her most talented because a man of the nature of Mendel Rivers wields the power he does. In short, the ideals of what I believe to be the single hope of mankind, the ideals of America, the promised land, might be so abused before the conditions are auspicious again that the ideals themselves might be forever tarnished.

We can meditate for a long while in our towers about what underlies the urgent character of events today. The self-congratulation of post–World War II America and the easy generalizations of anti-communism; the television mentality and weak public schools; the communications explosion; the nuclear age: the underlying causes are complex. But regardless of their nature and their relationship one to another, they have culminated in an America which must change in 1968 and might not live to see 1972 without that change. It must change and yet it can't without some frictions someplace. It won't change, in our opinion, unless something drastic is done. Civil disobedience as a manifestation of conscientious dissent is that drastic something.

As a political act, civil disobedience makes no pretense to being constructive. It is destructive in that it hopes by its agitation to shock America into a realization of its role in the world by destroying its illusions about itself. It is destruction, though, not of the system, but of abuses of the system, of misconceptions within it. In political terms it is not revolutionary. In personal terms civil disobedience is neither constructive nor destructive, it is simply refusal to comply, withdrawal to the side, opting out. As such it is an act of conscience, a drawing of the moral line of personal behavior across which one will not pass. Though, I must grant, many of my peers are less than judicious in their drawing of that line, and though they obviously defeat their own ends by the manner in which they draw it upon occasion, it must be noted that these people all assume that America is on a collision course with itself, and that collision is imminent. Thus the wonder is that the radicals about which Mr. Kennan pontificates are merely radicals and not revolutionaries in every sense of the word.

Today's youth in America is not revolutionary because it has lived outside the cloister of ideology to which Mr. Kennan would confine it. The political pragmatism which reflects their personal ambivalence toward political systems manifests itself in the fact that they do not appeal for a new system, as Mr. Kennan would naively encourage, but rather accept this system as the best possible under all the given circumstances — and so accept prison rather than pistols in order to preserve at least in terms of their personal behavior that system. This pragmatism, though, does have limits. Those limits are defined by the ideals which we refuse to drag down. And these ideals are for us young people what America is.

Thus conscientious dissent by civil disobedience today says that a national emergency exists which threatens everything which is dear to a believer in the true America, that there exists no present alternative within the system given the men in the system and their powers, that no amendment to the system could be effected in time to change things sufficiently to avoid the cataclysm, that the only possible alternative near the system is civil disobedience and creative destruction (obstruction), and that regardless of any political effectiveness, civil disobedience as an act of conscientious dissent is an act which will at least leave one's conscience clear amidst the turmoil of world and civil war.

Mr. Kennan's legalistic concerns will earn him the scorn which history will someday heap upon those who worried in 1968 about the American political institution and the sanctuary of the ivory tower when the American ideal of life, liberty, and the pursuit of happiness was suffering an apostasy.

Sincerely,
CURTIS M. DOWDS
Yale '68

Williamstown, Mass., January 21, 1968

To the Editor:

George Kennan's article ("Rebels Without a Program," Jan. 21) does a disservice to those concerned students for whom civil disobedience means non-violent non-cooperation rather than violence. By identifying civil disobedience with the "angry militants," Mr. Kennan overlooks the possibility of breaking the law as a moral duty. No doubt he is thinking of student demonstrators blocking campus recruiting, but what of inductees who must either go to prison or fight a war which they believe to be morally wrong? The purpose of refusing to cooperate in an unjust policy is twofold: first, to avoid involvement in the commission of injustice and, second, to cause other citizens and the leaders of the nation themselves to realize their error. While for the latter purpose civil disobedience may prove ineffective as a tactic, the former will nevertheless require it as a duty to one's conscience.

As Mr. Kennan says, civil disobedience is never a citizen's right. But, in the words of Thoreau, "I think we should be men first, and subjects afterward." As long as men are capable of independent moral judgments, civil disobedience will have a place in a democratic society.

ROBERT HALLEM
Williams College

To the Editor:

Mr. Kennan's remarks in the Jan. 21 edition of the NY Times magazine was a most sophisticated attempt to discredit campus activists. The first part of his essay tries to convince the reader that the activist is grossly anti-intellectual. Mr. Kennan accuses activists of "screaming, throwing stones, breaking windows, overturning cars," yet these generalizations are more applicable to the Ft. Lauderdale junior jet set. Most student demonstrations are non-violent; however, across the nation, it has been the police who have demonstrated barbarism, not the activists. Furthermore many studies have shown that student activists have more distinguished academic records than their quiescent colleagues. The July 1967 edition of the Journal of Social Issues reports that activists not only have more distinguished academic records but also are more altruistic and more favorably disposed to the arts than their peers.

Mr. Kennan also writes that there is "a serious doubt whether civil disobedience has any place in a democratic society." An activist might not agree with this statement but he will certainly disagree with the assumption that the United States is a democratic society. There has never been democracy in the South. Indian-Americans whose populations have been genocidally decimated by white Americans live in degrading conditions as do Negro-Americans in the North. College student dissenters at Brooklyn College, Wisconsin and elsewhere have been dealt beatings by local police forces.

That America is a democratic society has been repeatedly pounded into our brains in each and every year of elementary and high school education to an almost Pavlovian familiarity. The activist is no longer conditioned to false notions. The student activist wants a *real* democratic society. The question he faces is "Does civil disobedience have a place in a 'semi-democratic' society?" He answers with an unequivocal YES.

IRVIN SCHONFELD
Brooklyn College

Chicago, Ill., January 24, 1968

To the Editor:

Will someone tell George Kennan that the young people whose photographs he sees daily "being beaten or dragged about by the police" don't take their activities to be any more conducive to good scholarship than he. The point is that they protest despite the deprivation. Mr. Kennan urges a picture of the self-indulgence of the young. What of their self-sacrifice? Would he have had those student activists of Tsarist Russia devote their university years to "quiet and successful study" and leave the Tsar to carry on?

JARRETT LEPLIN, Instructor
Department of Philosophy
Illinois Institute of Technology

Dear Mr. Kennan:

Father Hesburgh has passed on to me, a student at Notre Dame, your comments in the *New York Times* of Jan. 21. I feel called upon to reply for two reasons. First, because I am the "type" at whom your cogent and convincing article was aimed: namely, one of the great many students who has thus far resisted any complete "surrender" to the tendencies of the New Left, but who find them interesting and ever more attractive. Second, I reply because I find in your remarks a microcosm of the great paradox we students see in our parents' generation. How can you provide us with the unbelievable opportunity of a place like Notre Dame and four more or less carefree years to imbibe of the wisdom she offers, and then become critical and distrustful of the "product"? How can you simultaneously have the good faith in our generation to seek the dialogue and cooperation for which your article pleads, yet feel threatened by our appearance and deportment in pursuit of and witness to the truth?

One point on which I am in complete disagreement with your article is in its espousal of the Wilsonian ideal of a university. Granted this vision provides a dramatic and eloquent preface to your remarks, it is far from Notre Dame's ideal and mine. Can this medieval concept be still pertinent after centuries of development in the ideas of both the university and its function in society? Father Hesburgh has called a university "a microcosm,

71

a place where all the tensions of the time tend to focus
. . . the fact is, it is a lively place." I wholeheartedly
agree, to the extent that I am more worried by the ap-
parent apathy at Notre Dame than by the negligible
"turmoil." Perhaps Father Hesburgh privately shares
this worry. At any rate, what we fear most is stagna-
tion, complacency.

Looking out from the Golden Dome, we see social
regimentation, conformity, and a herd mentality in
American society. To this we much prefer even the filtered confrontation of ideas and persons at a place such
as Notre Dame. Here we are *alive* and today this is not
proven by Descartes's *cogito* as much as by an existen-
tialist *patescor*. In earlier times man might have felt
most vital in serene contemplation of himself and his
own reason. But serenity is death; life is love and love
is terror and anguish and involvement and passion. That
the affairs of our time can be discussed "with knowledge
and without passion" seems most undesirable if not a
contradiction in terms. By this we do not mean "screaming tantrums and brawling in the streets . . . eyes
glazed with anger." (Perhaps in my sheltered existence
I have not been on the right campuses to observe this
phenomenon, but I see here a dramatic hyperbole. I
have in mind the notion of passion as it is generally applied to Socrates.)

Perhaps the best place to join forces with your generation is in mutually deploring hatred, intolerance, angry militancy and self-righteousness. We pledge to do
our part to cure this evil within our ranks by the only

effective means, ceaseless attempts at loving communication. We cannot see this problem, however, as a phenomenon peculiar to students.

Your observation that demonstrators are not really students is sometimes valid, but it obscures the equally valid danger that in our complex society wisdom may be drowning in a tidal wave of knowledge. Do you require that one spend four silent, uncritical years memorizing the intricacies of the American economic system, or nuclear physics, or the processes of the human body before earning the right to comment on the use to which this knowledge is put by our society? And more importantly, doesn't experience show that familiarity with one of these disciplines often precludes objectivity and brings on the tendency to substitute such knowledge for wisdom?

We know knowledge is necessary and useful in solving tactical problems, but the need for strategists is as always the more crucial. Not all study is the joyless drudgery described in your article. Certainly the quest of specialized knowledge demands discipline and detachment, and it therefore amazes me how many of my colleagues so readily relate to problem solving and plunge into the books and formulas night after night. Most of these are indeed "reserving judgment while evidence is accumulated." But I suspect the "accumulation of evidence" might just still be going on when someone pushes the button.

The reason so many of us seem to have or make time to demonstrate or write letters like this is that we have

73

been rewarded in our efforts to find teachers, perhaps only two or three in our college careers, who offer us not just knowledge but wisdom. We discovered the joy of learning and the ease with which truth is pursued. We began to see the folly in ourselves as well as others. We sense that most men acquire a fear of the truth, that if not exposed to it early in life they develop their "selves" as the basic criterion of meaning, and begin to evaluate new ideas by whether or not they threaten their hardening but always fragile little structures.

Perhaps this applies to your analysis of why we reproach you for "compromise." For you have in our eyes done more than compromise. You have subjugated things you knew or should have known to be right in order to fit in and be accepted. Many of us will do the same, no doubt. But perhaps we will at least spare ourselves the pathetic rationalization. For we know that idealism does not flag; it lives or dies. Polonius was an old father, yet he could see that ultimate responsibility to others does not, cannot conflict with responsibility to oneself and the truth. We do not agree that our maturity was made possible by our parents' materialistic faint-heartedness. We cannot other than impute to your generation the best of intentions and a tragic knack for rationalizing in this matter.

To me the most shocking statement in your article is that "the decisive seat of evil in this world . . . is simply in the weakness and imperfections of the human soul itself." Every fiber of my being, every holy and intimate experience I have known cries out against it and

74

shudders at the possibility of its truth. Great courage would be required for me to live in the belief that man himself is even less perfect than the political and social structures he has pieced together.

Inherent in your analysis of the error of drug use is a denial that this question is still open to research and discussion. My limited experience with those who have taken drugs leaves me uncertain that the marvelous resources within a man cannot be released through "passive submission to stimuli." I suspect that much of the creative and constructive thought of our age has been facilitated by drug experience. A minor but familiar case in point is John Lennon, an unabashed user and proponent of marihuana, who has moved from "She Loves You, Yeah, Yeah, Yeah" to the lyric poignancy of "Eleanor Rigby," "A Day in the Life," and "The Fool on the Hill." Reading these leaves me certain that his pose of deeper awareness is not fraudulent. Also, from what I can gather, the use of drugs is anything but a passive experience. Under their effect one's attention span is shortened, enabling the mind a grasp the ramifications of an idea and the meaning of these ramifications in turn without boggling. Perhaps this explains why drug use is most common and least criticized by those who set high value on dialectic thinking. At any rate, intelligent drug users maintain there is more to it than mere passive sensate experience. Other questions which seem unsolved are whether one has a "psychic equilibrium," whether this can be and is in fact "upset" by drugs, and whether it is definitely wrong to do this. A distinction

between "artificial" and presumably natural means of re-
leasing creativity and achieving awareness leads to a debate closely paralleling the birth control issue within the
Church, a question few on either side of the issue will
deny to be in a state of flux.

I agree that all freedoms bring with them responsibilities. Yet these obligations are neither burdensome
nor painful when the ideals for which they are under-
taken are not lost sight of. As long as we keep our eyes
on ideals such as love and wisdom, the pursuit of these
things, however outwardly arduous, is a genuine joy.

If we seem to be selfish, callous, and irresponsible, it
is truly a tragedy, for we do not appear so to one another. Let both generations indulge in earnest self-exam-
ination, imputing the best of faith to one another before
examining where our differences lie. A sure sign that this
goodwill is lacking is the ability to pity another man.
Our generation does not pity yours; we cannot pity and
respect at the same time. We do not fear you; we cannot fear and love at the same time. Actually we can fear
neither ideas nor our responsibilities to them as long as
we remain open.

You accuse us of cruelty to our parents. Were it
kinder to conform to a vision as meaningless to us as
ours apparently is to you? Do we demonstrate true love
and respect by pretending to agree with you? Are you
really hurt to see one of us following his own conscience? Can you not glory with us in our commitment
to a vision? That you feel threatened is perhaps unavoidable, but it is not our aim. We do not need your

trust in us but we want it and believe you could grant it, as many in your generation have done.

To accuse us of poor citizenship because we choose to demonstrate our concern by civil disobedience implies a similar narrowness in the definition of patriotism. For us, to choose a democratic system is not to accept all its workings, administrative and legislative, without question. The essence of democracy is not, for us, the willingness to accept the dictates of the majority, but the readiness to respect and defend the dignity and rights of the many minorities. Most of us believe strongly in the democratic ideal thus started, and in fact hold it to be the most free and viable system yet conceived and implemented by man. Yet even we must admit that in recent years the gap between this ideal and the practice in our land has assumed yawning proportions. Minorities are systematically ignored and oppressed, officials are corrupt, free thought is attacked where not stifled, leadership is untrustworthy; in short, revolutionary forces have been bottled up. But you realize this and admit it. You call us rebels without a program, but we are rebels because there is no program. Students are not and have never been charged with the responsibilities of leadership. Student dissenters do not incur "the obligation of saying in what way this political system should be modified." *Your* generation incurs this obligation — whether or not it thinks or dissents. We know the value of experience and maturity, we shun the demagogues of our own generation; we want leadership, we will respect and follow leadership that is creative and dynamic. My generation literally cries out to yours for a direction in which to prove our idealism and energy. You feign ignorance of our ideals, yet your remarks indicate to me, Mr. Kennan, that you are an acute observer, that you surmise what changes we would make if we could. Before deploring the noise, violence, and recklessness you see about you, think of what brought this on. Laws are not sacred, Mr. Kennan; people are.

In conclusion I want to thank you for your insights into both your generation and mine, for sharing the blame with us, for taking the first step toward dialogue and cooperation.

Yours,
JAMES L. FULLIN, JR.
Notre Dame '68

Ithaca, N.Y., January 23, 1968

To the Editor:

Mr. Kennan's article about the relationship between detachment and genuine scholarship has certainly been needed for a long time. It is an article which I hope everyone in the New Left will read with care. The ultimate truth of what Kennan says I cannot deny, but an indication of causes for the loss of detachment is, I fear, absent from his analysis.

Students today are increasingly faced with the knowledge that their scholarly pursuits are strictly limited, that soon they will be forcefully taken to perform menial tasks to contribute to a war they dislike. Or worse, they know they may be put into a position of sacrificing their lives for what they see as rather nebulous and hardly noble goals, pursuant to a policy which they find abhorrent and in which they seem to have no voice. It is extremely difficult to maintain a sense of detachment with one's thoughts subject to constant interruption by such prospects.

The presence of those who profit by deluding others is another disruptive force on campus. Among these pushers I include not only those who sell drugs which lead to a retreat from reality but also those who come with a propaganda message, not with a deep concern for the truth. Recruiters, particularly those of the military, come with such an aim. Military men are trained in the art of warfare, their recruiters, perhaps in the art of rhetoric, but not in the quest for truth; their presence, then, is just as destructive to a sense of detachment as the presence of those "students" whose primary concern is commitment, regardless of the truth of what they are committed to. Perhaps the very openness of the modern academic community has been partly responsible for this crisis in scholarship: one must expect that encroachment by the outside world will have its effect by making students aware that they are not detached.

One also wonders at the priorities of the government which commits crimes against scholarship by channeling it according to their wishes. They permit those whose goal is to delve into the intricacies of nature (usually called scientists) to continue their education because the products of such tinkering are immediately accessible and important: they lead to better bridges, television sets, and bombs. But those dedicated to the discovery of human truths, hopefully leading to understanding and peace — a task which requires far more detachment — are forced to live with constant uncertainty.

One must certainly admire a man like Mr. Kennan who can remain detached. Even though many, for various reasons, feel more attraction to commitment than detachment, those of us who prefer the latter often cannot find it. This summer I will be faced with the decision of whether to accept the duties this society demands, and deny my conscience, or to do something else, and perhaps lead a life of great trial and difficulty thenceforth. Facing such alternatives as these, detachment is a difficult road to follow.

The modern university often sees itself, as does the outside community, as a service institution for the community, rather than a place where pursuit of truth and knowledge, simply, is the highest end. This explains the current vogue emphasizing science; it explains the presence of recruiters; and, it also explains why there are draft deferments. Perhaps the real source of the crisis today is that our massive multiversities are becoming mere vocational schools, instead of places for consideration of the eternal questions and truths about man.

Mr. Kennan described the symptoms of what I, with him, consider to be a crisis in scholarship. What remains to be done is to suggest a means of re-creating the genuine student, that is, to provide an atmosphere where detached, leisured pursuit of truth and knowledge is once again possible.

ROBERT L. OAKLEY
Senior in the Department of Government
Cornell University

Toronto, Canada, January 25, 1968

To the Editor:

George Kennan's article of January 21 is quite disturbing. Its advocacy of a university nun-like in its "withdrawal and renunciation of participation in contemporary life" seems to me to be a dangerous ideal. Dangerous because in its "remoteness from the contemporary scene" it suggests the possibility of the acquiescence by the university in the given conditions of contemporary life.

As a college student one is relatively free for at least once in one's life from conflicts of interest with the goings-on of society's more "practical" enterprises. For once the student is able to criticize those enterprises with the help of those ideals of coherence, meaningfulness, and beauty that are offered to him by his study of the past. When George Kennan suggests, however, the impossibility of this, of a person's being both an activist and a good student, one must ask him, "What evidence do you have to verify this claim? Are such students in fact doing less well in their studies than their non-activ-

81

ist fellows?" Kennan's speculation on this subject is not enough.

It is also true that certain aspects of the Kennan–Woodrow Wilson ideal of a university do appeal to activists. The opposition on campuses across the United States to military recruiting, to classified research, and to such companies as Dow Chemical suggests that these students want a university that is free from the demands of society that may interfere with its proper functioning. The Kennan university, so calm, so slow to take excitement has, over the last two decades, become very passive in its relation to the outside world and its demands.

The problem with Kennan's article is its refusal to consider any specific arguments, inferences, conclusions, etc., of the student left. When he claims that they lack a program, does he mean that they have never suggested programs or that the programs they suggest cannot work, are immoral, would make matters worse? The difference is important. Kennan offers only melancholy sentiments; the university ideal is to argue specifics. In its dreamy reverie, so devoid of such specifics, Kennan's essay approximates Wilson's heaven-gazing academy. The result is that it becomes irrelevant to the problems of the earth.

T. H. ADAMOWSKI
Department of English
Erindale College, University of Toronto

To the Editor:

I have just read, with interest, Professor Kennan's article "Rebels Without a Program," as noted in *The New York Times Magazine*, 1–21–68, p. 23. I think his point on Wilson's conception of learning is as valid as his point on civil disobedience is invalid.

First, I find acceptable his statement of the civil disobedience position: "Some people, who accept our political system, believe that they have a right to disregard it and to violate the laws . . . so long as they are prepared, as a matter of conscience, to accept the penalties established for such behavior," *Times*, p. 71. Second, it is true that the "privilege of lawbreaking [is] preferentially in the hands of the affluent." To a large degree the amount of justice that an individual receives depends upon his social position and the ability to pay for expert advice. Third, civil disobedience is not equivalent to lawlessness. It is a correct deduction from lawlessness, but *not* from civil disobedience, that "it would then be all right for a man to create false fire alarms or frivolously to pull the emergency cord on the train, or to do any number of other things that endangered or inconvenienced other people." Civil disobedience does not engage in covert maneuvers so as to "create false fire alarms," but openly states and argues against maintaining false fire escapes. Likewise, an individual is not acting "frivolously" if he is prepared to go to prison for openly stating his beliefs. This should be as true for student conscientious objectors as it is for a Quaker. Lastly, reduction of some of the "great and obvious evils" of our society should hardly be regulated by the criteria of "inconvenienc[ing] other people."

There is a categorical difference between offering oneself as a test case by openly stating responsibility for an overt violation of the law, and retroactively accepting responsibility for covert acts if apprehended later. Dr. Spock's recent indictment clearly represents the former case, and any criminal's truthful plea of guilty represents the latter case.

Thank you for taking the time to consider this letter.

Sincerely yours,
JOHN R. FITCH
Graduate Student
Syracuse University

New York, N.Y., January 30, 1968

To the Editor:

George Kennan's article "Rebels Without a Program" is a sad reflection of the generation gap; it reveals only too clearly, and unconsciously, that kind of sloppy thinking and 19th century Puritanical self-righteousness that the young are rightly rejecting. I include myself among the young (23) and among the rebels (having turned in my draft card) but I do not consider myself radical, in Kennan's sense of the word. According to his fuzzy thinking anything beyond legalistic, political thinking is automatically radical and violent and ugly.

Kennan starts with his ideal of the university: "the association of the process of learning with a certain remoteness from the contemporary scene"; he believes that the perspective gained from this withdrawal can be used once the withdrawal is over (I notice that he cagily does not concede that that perspective may, once the monastic seclusion is over, be used for action; he simply recognizes that there is a time for action and a time for thought — but isn't our problem in Vietnam today due to the fact that thought has *not* been joined with action, but separated as though they belonged to the two different spheres that Kennan puts them in; whereas Kennan urges us, the young, to think now and act later our government seems to be acting now and thinking — perhaps — (later). Kennan quotes Woodrow Wilson and bemoans the fact that "in place of calm science . . . we have people utterly absorbed in the affairs of this passing world." He also makes use of his religious image which serves him in good stead throughout the article. He laments that the eyes of the young are turned everywhere "but to heaven for the satisfaction of their aspiration." Is this religious metaphor meant seriously? Is Kennan trying to revive God again to solve our problems?

I had four years of college (at Harvard) and saw enough to realize that the sterility and dishonesty of the system was due to that very ideal of Wilson–Kennan's;

we do indeed have calm science and we do indeed have total contempt for the real world and students are indeed monks. And the result is not Truth but it is grade-grubbing, cynicism (getting away with half-truths on exams and papers as long as it pleases the professor), sterility (life is not to be lived, but analyzed and computerized), and conformity (follow the rules of learning, accept the world as it is, do not argue or express yourself).

Kennan then admits that those of the radical left who espouse violence and obscene slogans "constitute only a minority on any campus." But in his own special doublethink he does not really mean this since he goes on to say that "a great many students" are subjected to "various forms of pleasing temptations" (Jesus tempted) or are forced into "crises of conscience." What does Kennan mean? What are the temptations he talks of, since he admits that only a minority engages in violence, etc.? The temptations obviously don't seem to be having much effect. And what is wrong with "a crisis of conscience" since it hurts no one and can only serve to force the individual to decide for himself where truth lies? (students especially need more crises of conscience since they, of all citizens, consider themselves most often possessors of knowledge and greatness).

Kennan then gets his first dig in at the hippies and once more the doublethink comes out for he says that Wilson's ideal of detachment from the world "was one intimately and sternly related to the real world." Either one is a monk or one is *not* a monk, at least as far as

Kennan views the university; you can't be mostly a virgin.

Kennan then talks about the complexity of our society and states that one could spend years studying the problems of policy and "reserve judgment while evidence is being accumulated." Again, calm science. But it is science that has become man's worst enemy. And why should anyone wait while more evidence (people killed, cities bombed, troops increased, nuclear war threatened — in Vietnam — and black people humiliated, killed, and oppressed here, at home) is collected. There is plenty of evidence NOW. We do not have the luxury of waiting, in our monastic cells, studying the speeches of LBJ; people die, as time passes, and we study — not to mention that the world could come to an end while we study. It is the Victorian cry of a long-lost century: WAIT — detach yourself, take on the nun's garment, forget the world — WAIT, until you are married.

"The world seems to be full, today, of embattled students. The public prints are seldom devoid of the record of their activities." Doublethink. First he admits a minority and now the world is crawling with them. And why does Kennan point to the "public prints" (isn't there an old-fashioned twinge to his prose, as outdated and confused as his thinking?) as evidence of this teeming mass? Surely he realizes that the mass media are totally unreliable and distort at will — and I include in one bag the New York Times, The Daily News, The New York Post, Channels 2–4–5–7–9–11–13, and radio. In every case one scene of violence or one hippie

87

gets headlines and the thousands of peaceful protesters and non-violent rallies and square students and elderly men and women are ignored. It is a cold-blooded assassination of that Truth Kennan professes to be after. Is he taken in by such distortions? Did he see the April 15 march in New York, the October 20–21 rallies in Washington, the December 4 demonstration in a Brooklyn church? If he did, he would realize that the violent faction of the radical left is less than a minority; it is the shadow of a minority.

Kennan then pulls the humble bit that we should realize that we could be wrong and that we should "offer a prayer for forgiveness for the event that we prove to be mistaken." The peace movement knows it can be wrong; its members helped elect LBJ and remind themselves and others constantly of this grim irony. But they do not offer prayers and they do not raise merely timid voices about the war because they feel the war is wrong enough to demand action, as citizens. If one is to complain of lack of openmindedness then our government is to be blamed, not the peace movement. The peace movement is openminded enough to be behind Senator McCarthy AND support draft resistance AND claim that the North Vietnamese are human beings who may want to talk about peace with us. That is quite a broad spectrum of openmindedness. Johnson seems to have only one thought in *his* mind: victory.

Kennan indulges in some sanctimonious parent-talk and then gets to the hippies; again, his fuzzy thinking, since hippies have little to do with the radical left. I agree with some of his points about hippies: I find it sad that they have no drive to act in this world, and I agree that they can, at times, be irresponsible. But, for the rest, their passiveness, their self-involvement is to me far more sane than the competitiveness and hatefulness of our society in general. At least hippies live and act out ideals of happiness, tolerance and generosity. But Kennan gives them the treatment; he sounds from another century, once more. He can even use as argument against the hippies the following: "It is only through effort, through doing, through action — never through passive experience — that man grows creatively." Where does this leave that ideal of the ascetic scholar?

But Kennan tries to cover over his fuzziness. For he admits that the hippies might indeed, in an earlier age, have been monks or scholars BUT (and Kennan loves buts) they would have had to have accepted discipline either in serving God and other men or in searching for truth (I would add that hippies have as much chance of discovering truths, through their search for inner happiness and experience, as scholars do in all of their books and secondhand knowledge). And Kennan's old-fashioned Puritanism comes out once more in an ugly way for he says: "They would have accepted an obligation to cultivate order, not chaos; cleanliness, not filth; self-abnegation, not self-indulgence; health, not demoralization." It is sad that Kennan does not realize that Hitler might well have used the same words. Order is not necessarily good: the army is orderly, Madison Avenue is orderly, capital punishment is orderly. Cleanliness is certainly not either good or bad — unless one had a strictly Puritan, middle-class view of it. Self-abnegation is only positive if it follows self-approval; there is certainly nothing wrong with self-indulgence as long as it hurts no one else. Health is a nice thing to have but it is hardly an ideal to look for; demoralization is not the opposite of health. No, the monastic order is not the answer to our problems. What we need is sanity, not order; morally clean actions, not cleanliness; self-approval and self-understanding, not self-abnegation; commitment to make society healthy, not health.

Kennan brings in the generation gap when he talks of the cruelty to parents of the hippies; but it is safe to say that in nine cases out of ten it is precisely the cruelty of these parents to their children which has led them to become hippies. It is the kind of cruelty that Kennan shows in this article; it is the cruelty of the Monk, the Pedant, the Puritan, the Man who will not commit himself to act on what he believes.

He now talks about the indifference of the rebels to the political system of this country. Is that so alarming? Our political system has done terrible things and is doing terrible things today; we have dropped two atomic bombs on innocent people, we have ignored legislation to help black people, we are killing people now in a dubious cause. Our politicians belong to a system which is outside of morality; they do not really represent anyone except themselves and their changing desires; America overwhelmingly rejected the insanities of Goldwater and promptly got the insanities of his political twin.

90

And now Kennan says — well, if the system is imperfect you must have a program of your own to change it. If he means that the protest movement should literally draft constitutional changes, new legislation, etc., then I would say that most of us in the peace movement are not qualified. But if he means programs in a more general sense then the peace movement has done more than its share; we have asked for a stop to the bombing, we have asked for negotiations with North Vietnam and the Viet Cong, we have asked for a steady withdrawal of American troops from Vietnam; these are concrete programs, and they have been presented at "peaceful demonstrations accompanied by reasoned argument and discussion" despite Kennan's sneers to the contrary; these are programs that could, realistically, be started immediately. So do not blame us for lack of a program. If you will listen, Mr. Kennan, and if the press will listen, and if President Johnson will listen you will hear our program — and while you are listening try not to worry too much about the fact that the people who present these programs may be under 30, may not be experienced, may have beards and may occasionally smoke marijuana, may make love before they are married, may reject American commercialness and competitiveness — try to forget those things as you listen because those things are neither moral or immoral.

We do not simply have a "constructive concept of what, ideally, ought to be done" — more importantly, in this practical world of yours, Mr. Kennan, we have many constructive concepts of what ideally and PRAC-TICALLY ought to be done.

Your mounting intolerance and unfair thinking is coming to a climax. For now you say, about civil disobedience, that one does not have the right to break laws even if one accepts the punishment for breaking them. I cannot go deeply into this but, briefly: laws are not always normally sane and when they are insane man must break them (again, your Puritan bent — the law, or God, *must* be obeyed); we lawbreakers will accept our punishments to show that we believe in the principles of our democracy but we DO NOT by any means claim that we have a right to break laws simply because we will accept the punishments; we claim that we have the right to break these laws because they are morally wrong and illegal; we believe that we are just, until we are proven unjust; and, even in prison, we will believe we are just because man's law and man's sentence is irrelevant compared to justice and morality. You will not be able to prove us unjust and immoral; I am convinced of that, I have no doubt of that, I am proud of that and I will not pussy-foot around while evidence accumulates to say that we are JUST.

To show you how inconsistent and untruthful you are, Mr. Kennan, you take a totally false analogy. You say that:

"It would be all right for a man to create false fire alarms or frivolously to pull the emergency cord on the train or to do any number of other things that endangered or inconvenienced other people, provided only he

92

was prepared to accept the penalties of doing so. Surely lawlessness and civil disobedience cannot be condoned or tolerated on this ground; and those of us who care for the good order of society have no choice but to resist attempts at its violation, when this is their only justification."

It is pathetic. You know damn well that draft resistance endangers no one but the draft resister himself (who has the right to commit suicide or stand on his head if he wants to). You know damn well that we agree that such lawlessness as causing false alarms cannot be condoned. You know damn well because you say that we must resist civil disobedience when the "ONLY JUSTI–FICATION" is the willingness to be penalized. You know damn well there are other justifications. But you will not admit it; and you claim to be interested in truth.

And your final appeasement does not interest me. You do not need to waste space praising the sincerity and idealism, the "unwillingness to accept a meaningless life and a purposeless society" of the young, simply as an afterthought. And it would NOT be wonderful, as you claim it would be (like the flickering finale of a Chaplin movie), "if we and they — experience on the one hand, strength and enthusiasm on the other — could join forces." Once more you confuse mere description with value judgments. Experience, strength and enthusiasm are not *necessarily* positive things. The war in Vietnam is a direct result of Experience and Strength and Enthusiasm; Hitler and Stalin and every bigoted person in this country had (and have) all three traits.

93

We need humanity and morality and sanity in order to undo all that experience and strength and enthusiasm has done in this world.

NICHOLAS MACDONALD
Harvard '67

New York, N.Y., January 21, 1968

To the Editor:

Mr. Kennan, in his article on the New Left, makes us pity him as he says he pities us. He has confronted the same horrifying lack of sense in our social structure and twisted maze of politics as we have, but he is afraid to act against it and frightened when others do. He convinces himself through pale labels and phrases ("reasoned argument and discussion," "will of the majority," "established authority," "violence and lawlessness") that the present state of American society is the best we can hope for now, and that one shouldn't complain in too loud a voice. He is blinded by guilt about his own disaffection, which he cannot do anything about. Therefore, when he sees young people who have enough freedom within themselves to act in whatever way seems best to them, he is horrified. What really horrifies him is a lack, an impotence within himself.

Mr. Kennan would like to return to the peace of an earlier, less complicated life. But the vision of Woodrow Wilson was of an America which no longer exists. The university is not a sanctuary from the hassles surrounding its campus. We breathe the same polluted air walking across College Walk as we do walking down Broadway. We are not cut off from the problems the establishment tries to conceal by giving student deferments and pretending that college is a combination of study and happy times which end at graduation. Hopefully students who are aware of the need for change and of their ability to help cause it will continue their action after graduation, instead of being buried by an avalanche of confrontations that they ignored as students.

The government and the establishment would like us to demonstrate and protest — quietly, that is, so as not to make any threatening vibrations. But we are demonstrating, and intend to demonstrate, in a way that the government can neither applaud nor fail to notice. We want to cause discomfort among the apathetic because we want to cause change. The biggest struggle is to shock people like Mr. Kennan out of their smugness.

Sincerely,
BARBARA BERNSTEIN
SUSAN BROWN
Barnard College

Morgantown, W. Va., January 21, 1968

To the Editor:

It is sad that one of the most respected critics of our current foreign policy so little understands or appreciates his youthful allies. Professor Kennan's conception of the academic life, while perhaps being appropriate to the Institute of Advanced Study, appears wholly out of touch with the role into which higher education has been, in the main, cast by our society. It is quaint that he has not noticed that the undergraduate, if not the graduate, experience has become a social and economic recruitment mechanism, far more than a philosophic grove. It is quite important to have graduated from a good school, and to have made good marks and engaged in high status student activities, but it is not, in our society at large, expected that one should have become seriously concerned with truth. In fact, such a concern can interfere with the sort of budgeting of a student's time and energy which the attainment of semester hours, quality points, and Greek letters usually involves. The marching to this rhythm which we impose on the young does, to be sure, involve discipline, but the more gifted and sensitive of our young will sometimes hear other drummers.

That Professor Kennan can accuse the rebellious youth of violence for its own sake is absolutely astonishing. In his day, a student rioted in order to steal a coed's lingerie, or for the sheer exhilaration of rioting. Today, when government bureaus, or corporations, involved in the war, would use the campus for their own, shall we say non-academic, purposes, the violence produced by such travesty may be blamed on various causes, but never on the love of violence. It derives, in reality, from a hatred of the unjust violence in which we are, as a nation, tragically engaged. Rather than to blame the youth for lacking the blueprint for a new order, such as the blueprints offered by the radicals of his day, Professor Kennan should realize that it is to men of his knowledge and influence that the responsibility belongs for noticing the defects of the present order and offering constructive suggestions for change. It is not as despisers of democracy that we demonstrate. We protest because our faith in the democratic dream which he and other leaders of his generation bequeathed to us has been betrayed. We heard of a world order administered for all men by reason in accordance with justice. We protest that, upon graduation, we will have to face the choice, which our brothers from the ghettos and the woods have already faced, of prison, loss of citizenship, or participation in a manifest injustice. We regret that our government has substituted pride and brute force for reason, and ideology for international order.

We have not asked for the responsibility to sit in judgment upon our leaders. We have not asked that academia become enmeshed in political and social controversy. Nor have we requested the disenchantment with community that leads to privatism. But our leaders have repeatedly lied to us about the morality of their actions. And others have made academia the "factory" which Dr. Kerr pronounced it. The raw material being processed can hardly be expected to react with contemplation, though they may well react with escape. Kennan's final acceptance of guilt can hardly be convincing, until he understands better what the young radicals are saying and doing.

Sincerely,
TIMOTHY RAY
Graduate Student
West Virginia University

Notre Dame, Ind., February 6, 1968

Dear Mr. Kennan:

I would like to reservedly agree with the greater part of your article of January 21, 1968, "Rebels Without a Program." It does seem that a more informed and effectively rational approach to involvement in today's affairs would be more worthy of intelligent students. Passion and half truths create an emotional and probably incorrect approach to problems. Students who seriously want to create change will do it by being well aware of the changes needed and by enlisting the cooperation of the society in which they must occur. This raises the question of a "faint-hearted" and seemingly apathetic adult society. There must obviously be some reason that adults become tempered gradually, a reason probably very much bound up with the process of living. It would seem once again therefore that the true nature of idealism is to be shaped by living, but in doing that, to come more quickly into contact with objective reality, realizing the true nature of life and living's practical limitations. If students could accept this fact and approach issues with a worldly wizened idealism, while we still have the vigor of youth, this combination of energy and effective practical wisdom will actually accomplish more than idealism out of touch with, and not in consideration of the everyday reality of living for most people.

I hope you and other concerned men of affairs won't be driven to "the other side of the barricades." Discord probably won't benefit either side as cooperation would. Age will probably put most of us, eventually, on what would be your side of the barricade, and we'll curse ourselves for this unthinking havoc we have wrought. This is not to give ideals, but rather to ask you how we can best in a necessarily limited way effect them. Thank you for your concern and attention.

Sincerely,
Bruce Boyle
Notre Dame

Cambridge, Mass., January 22, 1968

To the Editor:

I wish to jump to the defense of the youth first bitterly attacked and then sympathetically, almost pathetically consoled by George F. Kennan.

Mr. Kennan speaks as a bewildered father who is both deeply puzzled and almost unconsciously angered by children who do not conform to his notions of proper behavior. This bewilderment leads the distraught parent to at once unreasoningly lash out and at the same time excuse his madness by what is obviously a deep love for his offspring. In his anguish to admonish and cajole, in his anxiety to preserve his values and ideals, Mr. Kennan often violates the dictums he recommends to a less cool-headed, and less patient younger generation. Maybe the young are unwise; maybe they should be patient, but time and the confusion of events do not wait upon "years of discipline and restrained study, years of scholar's detachment, years of readiness to reserve judgement while the evidence is being accumulated." The evidence is never in, Mr. Kennan. Five years ago he would never have publicly advised Martin Luther King to restrict his efforts in persuading Alabama to vote his freedom, nor ask the Carolina Negro college students to leave the lunch counters and return to their campuses for well-argued, heavily footnoted debates. The injustices they fought cried for remedies which could not wait upon (a perhaps never arriving) democratic solution. America's Asian war, America's poverty, and her ghetto chaos strike young militants as similarly pressing problems for which immediate action is needed. I along with Kennan pray that America will survive the sickness and its cure.

But differing from Mr. Kennan, I cannot plead for the sanctity of the university. Its walls block out as much as they let in. Princeton is hardly a place from which to look out on changing America. Taking a bit of his own advice Kennan ought to study the militants he so dislikes. They come in many different varieties. Some, as he points out, are doctrinaire and rigid. But a perusal, for instance, of the writings of the Students for a Demo-

100

cratic Society (S.D.S.) would reveal young men and women searching for modes of "political reform," searching for a way to make modern democracy workable and meaningful. They are hardly, as he labels them, "Rebels Without a Program." Mr. Kennan should reread the first part of his quote from Woodrow Wilson. These same students whom he views from across a generational gap are trying in the university to be "debaters of the world's questions every day and used to the rough ways of democracy." It was an attempt to fulfill this part of Wilson's vision that brought students who had little control over their fates into conflict with the Berkeley administration and gave rise to the Free Speech Movement. The desire to speak for their lives and practice the "rough ways of democracy" leads students to sit-in, expose secret government research on campuses, and burn their draft cards.

If these same militant students alienate the generation of George Kennan, if they appear cruel to their parents through lack of filial piety, then one might look at what Mr. Kennan's generation stands for both as political actors and parents. Though Kennan may be above reproach, the sons who watched Adlai Stevenson lie in the U.N., read Schlesinger's White Paper on Cuba, saw Kennedy appoint racist judges in the South, viewed Vietnam and Santo Domingo, these sons lose faith in their fathers, lose faith especially when, as Kennan does, the fathers claim the weight of their personal responsibilities as an excuse. Are thirty thousand dollars a year income, two cars, a surburban house, Harvard and European

101

vacations an argument for parental noninvolvement? Children don't ask for this. A state university, an apartment in the inner city, and public transportation never deprived a child of any of the real advantages of life. If there appears to be a lack of love on the part of children, this is a consequence of parental incapacity to understand that their militant offspring do not want sterile advantages, do not want conformity; they want to change the world and they are not afraid of being impolite.

Having rambled at length, this aging youth (almost past the age of trust) would like to apologize to Mr. Kennan. I do not mean to direct my comments to him personally. His angry outburst prompted my equally angry retort. I am trying to say to Mr. Kennan that my world of S.D.S., Stokeley Carmichael, Robert Sheer, F.S.M., and Staughton Lynd, like his, is not blind and totalitarian, but has some sense and reason, some urgency and coherence, some love and piety on its side.

CHARLES S. FISHER
Assistant Professor of Sociology
Brandeis University

III

LETTERS FROM THE
OLDER GENERATION

New York, N.Y.

To the Editor:

There is no one in public life for whose integrity and wisdom I have greater respect than Mr. George Kennan but in his otherwise excellent article occurs a passage which, coming from him, alarms me considerably: "These observations reflect a serious doubt whether civil disobedience has any place in a democratic society. . . . Some people, who accept our political system, believe that they have a right to disregard it and violate the laws that have flowed from it so long as they are prepared, as a matter of conscience, to accept the penalties established for such behavior. I am sorry, I cannot agree. . . . It would then be all right for a man to create false fire alarms or frivolously to pull the emergency cord on a train . . . provided he was prepared to accept the penalties of so doing."

Mr. Kennan is far too intelligent not to know that his example is a red herring. Who ever heard of a man going to the police and saying: "I have just turned in a false fire-alarm. Please arrest me"?

I commit an act of civil disobedience if I deliberately break a law because I believe it to be unjust, either negatively or positively. A negatively unjust law — the Prohibition law of the twenties, for example (passed, by the way, "democratically") — is one which *forbids* an action which should be a matter of private, not public, judgment. A man who went to a speakeasy or dealt with a bootlegger did not say to himself: "It is my moral *duty* to drink whiskey." He said: "I have as much moral *right* to drink whiskey as my neighbor has to drink milk."

In the case of a negatively unjust law, a man will break it as privately as possible; he has no intention of paying the penalty if he can possibly avoid it because he thinks the state has no moral right to exact one.

A law is positively unjust if it *commands* an action which is unjust or immoral. A man who publicly refuses to serve in the armed forces, as distinct from a draft dodger, does not say: "I have a *right* to defy the law." He says: "It is my *duty* to defy the law. Moreover, though the majority do not yet recognize it, it is really the duty of *all* men to defy it." It is only in such circumstances that a man can be said to "accept" the penalty for defiance.

To claim that one is right and the majority wrong is, of course, morally perilous; every crank and megalomaniac is prone to make it. But to suggest, as Mr. Kennan seems to, that the claim can *never* be justified is to deny that human history owes anything to its martyrs. Dr. Johnson, who was certainly no anarchist, thought otherwise:

"The magistrate has a right to enforce what he thinks, and he who is conscious of the truth has the right to suffer. I am afraid there is no other way of ascertaining the truth but by persecution on the one hand and enduring it on the other."

W. H. AUDEN

Princeton, N.J., January 26, 1968

To the Editor:

George Kennan's "Rebels Without a Program" is appalling. There is barely a sentence in the article free of false accusation, self-enclosed argument, misplaced indignation. It is a gross misrepresentation of the radical left on the campus, just the sort of patronizing and distorted account which helps to confirm 20-year-olds in their view that "liberals" are incapable of understanding either the new generation or the new problems which confront our society. It is, moreover, a dangerous article, for it lends the weight of Kennan's name to a perspective and a rhetoric more usually associated with a Ronald Reagan — though I do not doubt Kennan would deplore the repressive policies which that rhetoric is likely to encourage.

I cannot believe that Kennan has read extensively in the position papers frequently issued by Students for a Democratic Society (S.D.S.), the national organization which represents radical left opinion on the campus. If he had, he could not possibly refer to their "massive cer-

107

tainties," their "screaming tantrums," their consuming interest in "violence for violence's sake," etc. I have often argued with S.D.S. members over particular points or attitudes, but never because I found them naïve utopians or romantic perfectabilitarians. On the contrary, S.D.S. members I have known at Princeton are far more knowledgeable and sophisticated, far less imprisoned by myth and ideology, than is the average undergraduate. Because they believe there can and should be less suffering in the world, hardly makes them utopians.

True, they have no "blueprints" for creating a better world. If they had, the charge of naïveté *would* apply, for only a simpleton (or a Marxist) would pretend to have a detailed set of answers for the multiple evils which face the modern world. It's the old story: when radicals do produce plans for a better society, they are denounced for attempting to straitjacket fluid reality; when they fail to produce plans, they are denounced as visionaries. Those who oppose substantive change can always find some reason for doing so.

But let there be no pretense that youthful radicals have no line of argument. If Kennan will read the literature written by members of S.D.S., he will find any number of proposals for "constitutional amendment or political reform" as well as that very wealth of "reasoned argument and discussion" he claims does not exist. I find it sadly amusing that the sole positive proposal Kennan himself offers to meet that national crisis which he does admit is upon us, is a "readiness to join" discontented youth in an "attempt to find better answers." Apparently

108

then, Kennan himself, despite forty years more experience than today's college generation, has no solution for the country's ills. By what right, then, is he so sternly critical of the undergraduates' "lack of program"?

A few other points: 1. *Kennan's view of the expert's role in public policy.* Though he scorns those non-democrats who believe society "ought to be governed by enlightened minorities," he seems to fall within that category himself. On top of his belief that experts should make policy, he also implies that only experts are fit to comment on it (policy matters are so complex, he writes, that they cannot be understood without "years of disciplined and restrained study"). The implications of this position are horrendous. We would have to discount an average man's simple outrage at the horrors of the ghetto, for example, as mere "emotionalism," as, given its lack of scholarly detachment, something of an impertinence. 2. *Kennan's views on education.* In Kennan's 18th century rationalist eyes, education takes place in direct proportion to the absence of emotion (indeed, of any kind of commitment, even intellectual). This is to confuse mere fact-gathering with true education (that is, self-discovery), a process which can hardly take place unless the whole person, emotions and all, is engaged. Kennan's views do fall within the mainstream of American educational philosophy and practice, which is to say, he shares the majority's misreading of why and how people learn and what knowledge is for. 3. *Kennan's view of "evil."* "The decisive seat of evil," he tells us (the philosopher briefly giving way to the Calvinist), is in "the weakness and imperfection of the human soul itself." Would that the behavioral scientists knew as much of human instincts and motives as Kennan seems to — though they, at least, do not pretend to. If members of S.D.S. used the vague, un-scientific, un-documentable terminology that Kennan does (e.g. "the infinitely delicate balance that nature created in the form of man's psychic makeup"), they would deserve the epithets of naïveté that he hurls at them. Besides, I doubt if even Kennan would argue that institutional arrangements and the policies of statesmen have an insignificant effect on the amount of evil in the world — which is all that S.D.S., wisely eschewing metaphysical speculation on the contents of the human soul, claims.

To my mind this is the best generation our country has yet produced — for the reason that it contains a substantial minority who will not be deterred from asking whether established slogans and authorities really are advancing human happiness. The new generation is so good that I feel sure it will not let the slanders of a George Kennan unduly concern it.

Sincerely yours,
MARTIN DUBERMAN
Professor of History
Princeton University

Dear Mr. Kennan:

I have just finished your article in the Times Magazine, *Rebels Without a Program*. Because I so thoroughly respect your intelligent analysis of this country's history and policies, as well as your integrity when you choose to express yourself, I feel you will also listen carefully to those who come to you, no matter what age, to express their reasonable doubts about your opinions. Much of what you said in this article, I agreed with, but the conclusion which impresses me as the most important for every human being to understand expresses your faith in the family and the relationships within it, as the source either of tremendous individual strength and capability or if the relationships are unhealthy or the family broken, as a source of unnatural character development and individual doubt.

For someone of my age, thirty-one, this faith is essential to my whole life. I am the mother of four children, before I am anything else. I believe firmly that I must bring up my own before I can help others to solve their problems. I believe I can give my children what they need *because I was given it* — and by *it* I mean certain values, attitudes and above all else a sense of humor about oneself which will help them bear the recognition of their own limitations as they grow older and realize the world cannot be set straight by an single human being, no matter how well-intentioned.

But where we part company is, on first, the relation-

111

ship of parent to child — in particular a hippy's parent and his child. I have yet to *meet* a child who, having been given consistent daily attention and sympathy, prompted by love and an understanding of a parent's responsibilities, has turned on the parent and rejected him, and his standards, as these recent rebels and "hippies" sometimes have. And I will not reprimand the rebel. Their revolt and rejection against the materialism and disregard of their parents may seem cruel to you but to me it is understandable and even heartening. In some ways their set of values are much better than their parents. I have watched these bearded, beaded people with either their own children or others' children. They have a certain kindness and awareness of the simplest needs of a child — they are sensitive people, who are giving their own children the love and attention their parents may have been too preoccupied to give to them — and I do not mean by attention, a big room with toys, a daily bath, and a perfectly balanced diet. No child owes any parent anything — and this I truly believe — We give love and receive it because we want to — the infant does it by instinct — out of necessity — not because we ought to. No child turns from a loving parent — it is against nature. If "this golden chain of affection is broken" it is initially broken by the parent, maybe unconsciously, but it is the parent's responsibility to then try and repair it.

And here I come to the second objection to your article. I think you should expand the thought which is almost a plea — in your last sentence — How wonderful it would be — I sometimes think to myself, if we and they . . . could join forces.

We can. But we the parents have first to sympathize through direct contact with the needs of these young — to speak of them with real affection and a sense of humor — we must unbend and not talk of we and they, but admit that all of us have goofed from time to time — that we liberals love to posture about improving the lot of man, while we allow, without much resistance, actions which contradict our words — the generation of adults who thus seems so dishonest can hardly expect respect from a generation which sees the gap between preaching and action. Far better to stop trying to justify our questionable actions, in war, in business, and admit them to be what they are. And finally I think your Wilsonian definition of the ideal University is dated. It smacks of the Ivory Tower and no young person with intelligence and sensitivity today wants to breathe that rarefied air — that atmosphere can turn into just as dangerous an escape hatch as Greenwich Village, East. The world has changed since Wilson's day — you cannot remain detached in the same way, for the young man of today has a different set of circumstances to face. A young student at C.C.N.Y. told me all the so-called rebels are not irresponsible students. Often they are the brightest members of the class, with the most incentive and initiative — and they do learn. Where we skipped lectures to go to a silly but entertaining movie, they use their time to organize their dissent — their involvement in their times is much more intense, because the problems of their times are very serious. Thank God they feel strongly enough to express themselves. You would not want them to adopt middle-aged moderation, or expect the wisdom of an older man from a 20 year old.

Please listen more closely to the students — obviously there are rotten apples in their barrel too — and the violent ones and the drugged ones are not typical, but extremists. Please sympathize more with their sense of urgency, especially that of the Negro. They have only gotten halfway through their period of questioning and revolt. Now they need help to find the constructive action to justify it — from such men as you. Please write more and present the alternatives that you think are open to these people.

Your ardent admirer,
SHEILA NITZE

Middletown, Conn., January 22, 1968

Dear Mr. Kennan:

May I ask for clarification of a point which you made in the article, "Rebels Without a Purpose"? You said that some people use as an argument for civil disobedience the fact that they are willing to undergo punishment for violation of the law. That is, they have a right to break the law because they are willing to accept the consequences of their actions within the democratic framework. Now I agree with you that this argument

114

will not do. Indeed, I find it scarcely intelligible. But what worries me is that I have never heard anyone use this as a *justification* of civil disobedience. Those who broke the law in civil rights demonstrations and those who are now breaking the law in anti-conscription demonstrations appeal to a variety of principles, usually moral or religious, but never, as far as I know, to what I shall call the Principle of Consequences.

Perhaps two different points have been confused here.

1. Dissenters such as Spock, Coffin, and Levy appeal to values which they think transcend the State. The State is not the Absolute. Hence, for the dissenter, certain universal moral or religious principles *justify* his violation of the law.

2. The dissenter is, as a matter of fact, *willing* to accept the consequences of his actions within the democratic framework. This point distinguishes the dissenter from the deserter or the traitor. It distinguishes Thoreau from Benedict Arnold. It distinguishes the draft-dissenter from the draft-dodger.

It seemed to me that you confused these quite separate points in your article. Because no one uses (2) as a justification for civil disobedience, are you not attacking a straw man?

Sincerely,
ROBERT L. PHILLIPS
Lecturer in Philosophy
Wesleyan University

To the Editor:

George Kennan's article in Sunday's *Times* Magazine section is, as one might expect, brilliant, philosophic, and provocative. Its plea for a union of the enthusiasm of youth with the experience of middle age is forever timely. His arguments leading to that most acceptable conclusion, however, are wanting in several ways.

First, his portrayal of the detached disciplines of the university, based upon a statement of Woodrow Wilson at Princeton in 1896, is an ideal that is limited by its origin in a nineteenth century world removed even then from the reality of its times. Indeed, it has far more in common with the medieval combination of monastery and university than the twentieth century university which both in laboratory and in the social sciences owes much to Dewey's "learning by doing."

In his philosophic "objectivity," Mr. Kennan fails to see the realities of the situation of twentieth century university life whereby the pressures of government are evident in innumerable ways.

a. Research programs which absorb more and more of the energies of the university are increasingly the result of government grants, or of industry subsidized by or entwined with government, often the Defense Department.

b. CIA influence upon international student organizations has been far-reaching.

c. The university is usually a recruiting and training ground for the military.

d. The student's presence at the university is itself a privilege, granted by one's local draft board in accord with the sometimes vindictive directives of General Hershey.

e. Every male college student must come to a decision as to whether or not he should participate in a military action which many believe to be immoral, helpful to communism, and a threat to the existence of mankind.

f. More and more of our young people attend universities that are supported by public money and subject to public influence.

Thus, for reasons over which the student has no control whatever, the American university of today is not even remotely like the quiet, detached, pastoral world of Princeton in the 1890's. A Woodrow Wilson either of 1968 or 1920 would be unlikely to speak as he did in 1896.

Secondly, Mr. Kennan's discussion of law, despite his wisdom and helpful insights, leads me to ask: Have not the great advances in the laws of mankind been largely the result of drastic action? There would be no Sinai Covenant without the crossing of the Red Sea, no Magna Charta without the protests of the barons, no United States Constitution without the Declaration of Independence, and there was no 14th amendment until the Civil War.

Conversely, is it not also true that men usually lose

their liberties legally? I do not believe that President Johnson or any man wielding high civilian or military authority wills the weakening of the democratic process but great evils are often wrought by good men with good intentions who allow themselves to become victims of abstractions. Personally, I fear the loss of our liberties through a descent into fascism in strict accordance with law far more than I fear the protesting "lawlessness" of our youth. The erosion of the power of the Senate in foreign relations, the relentless growth of presidential power in all areas, the growing influence of the military in education, in industry, and in politics, the presidential usurpation of the power to declare war — these are and have been since ancient days the signs of the twilight or at least the afternoon of liberty.

The fact that many of our most sensitive, thoughtful young people do not know how to be enthusiastically constructive in their country's service is not their failure but ours.

Very truly yours,
NORMAN EDWIN THOMAS, D.D.
Minister, The First Church in Albany

Cambridge, Mass., January 23, 1968

To the Editor:
Mr. Kennan's brief against student radicals is put so eloquently that I fear some readers may not see it for what it is — the partisan support of an opinion. His ma-

118

jor thesis is that a portion of the student generation, having sacrificed the monastic learning of the ivory tower for mindless, anarchistic participation in the political arena, is no longer capable of being educated for a responsible role in our society. The evidence for this is in the writer's impression — apparently gathered from the mass media — of the behavior of student participants in acts of civil disobedience. But the inference that those who express themselves by physical rather than intellectual action are incapable of reason is inacceptable; they include, as the Justice Department has recognized, a number of mature scholars and scientists with unassailable intellectual credentials.

In my experience, the activists are often not only better and more imaginative students than others of their contemporaries, but have contributed significantly to enlivening and enriching the intellectual atmosphere in the universities by contrast to that of the passive and dreary years of the McCarthy era. Because they are in opposition, many of them are committed to a search beyond the preparation for examinations, and because they no longer accept traditional attitudes unquestioningly, they have challenged their teachers to articulate their own premises and convictions. Nor can I accept without evidence the proposition that the radicals act "with a minimum of knowledge." I know many who are better informed on political affairs than most of us, but I hesitate to claim with Mr. Kennan that such limited experience qualifies me to make valid generalizations.

I agree that recourse to illegal political and social action can be dangerous; but what of the dangers of President Wilson's "calm Science seated there, recluse, ascetic, like a nun" to which Mr. Kennan admiringly refers? Did the antiseptic science and scholarship of our generation really help the academy to formulate ideals for our future? It did not: the preponderance of learned journals and university press publications, and particularly those of the "humanists," have been technical exercises addressed by professionals to a small circle of colleagues rather than contributions to humane learning. If that sort of denial of responsibility and leadership is the alternative we offer in the name of discipline, dare we accuse the students of not being mature citizens and creative critics?

At this moment, it is by no means proven that the activists on one hand and the hippies on the other will become less valuable citizens than my contemporaries who swallowed goldfish and started panty-raids. For centuries, European students have been disruptive in similar ways, and western civilization has probably benefited more than it has lost from the recurring challenge.

Anyone who wants to help young people to articulate their passionate convictions rationally is headed for failure if he does not start from a positive assessment of the idealistic and creative aspect of their commitments. It is not our prerogative as elders to remake them in our own image; at best we may help them to find means of matur-

ing and structuring their own responses to the present
condition of man.

Sincerely yours,

JAMES S. ACKERMAN

Professor of Fine Arts

Harvard University

New York, N.Y., January 22, 1968

To the Editor:

Mr. Kennan's "Rebels Without a Program" is at the
same time deeply moving and deeply disturbing. I think
he is right in treating the "radical left" and the flower
people separately. I find that the radical left has a very
definite, though narrow program: stop the war in Vietnam, which the members find (and I believe rightly so)
immoral, outrageous and unjust.

The radical students are not confronted with a University which "sees the world go by," but instead find
recruiters of the armed forces, the recruiters of the
armament industry recruiting on campus, find (in many
instances) the military directly lecturing on campus
(ROTC!).

The sections on Civil Disobedience seem to miss the
point completely. Civil disobedience is often and seriously misused. It has a place where problems of conscience are involved, and in such cases is a right in the
deepest spiritual and religious sense and not a privilege
which the secular state, democratic or otherwise, can

121

grant or withhold. Thoreau is an outstanding example in our own history.

I agree completely with Kennan that "so much of the danger [for our country] comes so largely from within." Our society is desperately sick. The fact that this is hardly recognized by the "establishment" (government as well as our educational institutions) explains the hippie movement (which unfortunately does not even wish to explore suggestions for changes) and the "new left" which engages at least in part in irrational forms of protest. But we can complain about these movements only after we have started an open and deep discussion about the illness of our society. As long as we tolerate the hypocritical nonsense in federal and state pronouncements, as long as university administrations fear to discuss the present, we have little right to complain about the "wayward youth."

> Victor Paschkis
> Professor Emeritus
> Former Adviser to Quaker Students
> Columbia University

Cambridge, Mass., January 28, 1968

To the Editor:

In "Rebels Without a Program" (January 21, 1968), George F. Kennan divides student dissenters into two classes — political activists, who by their "screaming tantrums and brawling in the streets" make a mockery of scholarly ideals, and the "flower children," who in "their defiant rags and hairdos" have renounced all obligations to society in order to serve their appetites, commonly perverted by the use of drugs.

Both the types he describes exist and doubtless deserve the condemnation he dispenses. (It is also being dispensed, daily and nightly, by the news media, which never fail to move in with cameras and pejorative adjectives on the long-haired and short-skirted in anti-war demonstrations, and never, if they can help it, show or mention a middle-aged demonstrator or one wearing a necktie.) But it ignores the plight, if not the very existence, of those who matter most — the young men and women who thoughtfully, from principle, and with great courage have declared they cannot kill or abet killing, even when bidden to do so by their country, in a cause they believe is profoundly unjust.

Mr. Kennan is in effect saying that such young men and women (if any happen to exist) have no choice. They must do as bidden. If they will not, they do not deserve the respect, to say nothing of the support, of those of us who are not subject to such bidding.

This is a harsh judgment from one who has written so much and so sensitively about the horrors of modern war. In public testimony and in his brilliant *Memoirs* as a diplomat, Mr. Kennan has himself furnished many of the most telling arguments against our war in Southeast Asia: the ever-growing domination of all national policy — and hence of American life generally — by military requirements; the bugaboo of a monolithic Communist enemy that can be staved off only by sufficient millions of U.S. armed forces and megatons of armament permanently at the ready around the globe; the questionable value, even for military purposes, of massive bombing, not to mention its moral implications for those engaged in it; and much else that makes this particular war a kind of burlesque of all wars. Not in any comic sense of course, but in the extremity of its costs in blood and treasure, in corruption and cynicism, in bungling and futility — and all to bring democracy to a people who, rightly or wrongly, are at present little interested in our brand.

It is a realization of these irrecoverable moral and material costs that has prompted the thoughtful young dissenters to take their stand. Mr. Kennan argues that they have no ground to stand on unless they can present an alternative "program," and he perceives none. But is it not a program to urge that better things should be done with our vast but by no means limitless resources? Did not many of these same young men and women and others like them throw themselves into the work of bettering human conditions, in our own country and abroad, before the insatiable demands of this war frustrated their efforts, transferred the civil rights movement largely into the hands of the advocates of "black power," and converted the Peace Corps, at least in part, into a refuge from military service?

Finally, it seems to me, in his discussion of civil disobedience, Mr. Kennan is uncharacteristically bland and cocksure. He is "sorry" but he cannot agree that it "has any place in a democratic society." By this line of reasoning, any appeal from the authority of the state to a higher law of conscience can be admirable only if it took place either in the past or at a safe distance. Thus it may have been admirable in Socrates' Athens, Christ's Palestine, the England of More, Hampden, and the Puritans, and Gandhi's British India. It may still be so in the late Chief Luthuli's South Africa and in the Soviet Union of Pavel Litvinov and his friends who have just been tried and convicted in Moscow. But in the United States of America it can be neither tolerated nor its roots and meaning understood. The work of such Americans as Roger Williams, the men who wrote and voted for the Declaration of Independence, Thoreau, John Brown, Garrison, and Debs is entirely done and they have nothing more to say to us. If this is really so, then America is a finished nation in more senses than one.

L. H. BUTTERFIELD
Editor in Chief
The Adams Papers

Hyattsville, Md., January 22, 1968

Dear Mr. Kennan:

Thank you for your thought-provoking article in the New York Times Magazine of January 21. It was read with varying responses by my wife — human rights activist and assistant information officer with the Embassy of Japan, my daughter — student activist at Sarah

Lawrence College (just completed some sort of exchange course at Princeton), and myself — as an employee of the Social Security Administration in the Medicare program, the family's only working socialist (pragmatic).

None of us were in complete agreement — or disagreement. My own reaction was rejection of limiting the university to a quiet place of meditation, reflection and study in search of truth. This may be an ideal, but it seems to me that the world's really great universities are found in or near teeming cities — not in remote isolation. Perhaps the austere isolation of the monasteries was needed as a repository for history during the bleak centuries of the dark ages, but I simply don't think they would be relevant in today's world.

As I understand my daughter's reaction . . . during a three-way long distance (collect of course) discussion . . . her concern was with the inference of a lack of alternatives on the part of her generation. She has worked one summer with ghetto kids on an Upward Bound program and spent last summer working in Appalachia. As a result of her own experiences, an excellent drama student is shifting to economics with plans to go on to law school — due to a recognition of her lack of tools to resolve inequities.

And my wife's reaction dealt with the closing paragraphs. She got the impression that, in what seemed to be a latent resentment of the rejection of the heritage we have developed for our young activists, you almost identify with those who have gone the "drop-out" route.

126

Certainly we are in agreement that a government of law is preferable . . . but only so long as those laws are equitable to both the majority and the minority. Perhaps all three of us, as somewhat rejected white Mississippians, are oversensitive to the prostitution of those laws that the entire nation permitted and condoned for decades, in the sacred name of "preservation of law and order."

And now I am afraid. If our system is to survive, we no longer have the leisure of another hundred years or so to correct other inequities. Modern technology now brings the affairs of state into every home, regardless of how humble, just as they take place. My own opinion is that revolution grows — not in grinding oppression and hopeless poverty — but in frustrated aspirations. That state seems to me to be where we are today.

> Sincerely,
> ALBERT W. HEFFNER, JR.

Wheaton, Md., February 11, 1968

Dear Professor Kennan:

Your discussion of the quest for truth in your recent article "Rebels Without a Program" was particularly appealing to me, since I am a scientist by profession, and have perhaps a more emotional attitude toward truth and falsehood than some others. The falsehood that preoccupies me now is the whole justification for our Vietnam position put forward by our government.

I first became interested in this matter when I watched Senator Fulbright's Vietnam hearings. Astonished by the discrepancy between what I heard there and what I thought I knew of that unfortunate war, I began a program of reading which covered Fall, Lacouture, Halberstam, Shaplen, Kahin and Lewis, and many others. Most recently I read Stillman and Pfaff's *Power and Impotence*. It was profoundly dismaying to learn that the statements of our government about the war are a mixture of omissions, distortions and outright lies, and that for the past dozen years or so, we have been an outlaw nation.

I feel that the disaster of the Vietnam war would never have occurred had the people known the truth. This brings me to the central question. How can democracy function when the people are systematically misinformed by their government? What safeguards can be enacted to ensure that the people know the truth? I sometimes think that the existence of mass communications has greatly exacerbated the problem, since the government has so enormous and instantaneous a means of reaching the people. The increasing centralization of the communications industry, and its deepening involvement with defense industry means that the government has a greater control over the news, and dissent is less than ever able to be heard.

Some argue that the government has always misled the people, but it seems to me that the abuse is growing worse. Recent episodes — Mr. Rusk's contortions on peace feelers, or the denunciation by Westmoreland and Bunker of Communist treachery after we had canceled the Tet truce on less than one hour's notice — are so flagrant, and so inept, that one feels that our officials are flaunting their disregard of truth.

In my gloomier moments, I wonder whether they have all gone mad, and can no longer distinguish between truth and lies, or have perhaps mastered Orwell's appalling art of doublethink. (If there is an afterlife, the late Mr. Orwell must be deriving a sardonic satisfaction from the verification of his dreadful predictions.)

But to return to a more constructive attitude, how can one prevent the occurrence of a credibility gap of the magnitude of this one, which has led the nation to its present unhappy and imperiled state?

Must one hire advertising firms to "sell" the truth to a society increasingly based on illusion?

I address these questions to you because I feel that they are intimately bound up with the question of civil disobedience which you discussed in your article. I have never been able to formulate my position on this matter, but have always fallen back to the unsatisfying answer that each case must be decided on its merits. For example, I feel that a Negro in Alabama would have been quite justified in violating a segregated seating law in Alabama, because Alabama was not a democracy as far as he was concerned. Now I wonder whether the systematic lying by the government has so debased the democratic process that civil disobedience is again justified. (I refer to peaceful civil disobedience only, not violence.)

Forgive me for burdening you with so long a letter, and thank you once more for your kind reply, and for the calm illumination which your writings shed on our troubled affairs.

Sincerely yours,
ROSALIND B. MARIMONT

Delaware, Ohio, January 28, 1968

To the Editor:

I was impressed — and disturbed — to discover the extent to which George Kennan misreads the current unrest among young people ("Rebels Without a Program"). Like so many others, he judges the whole by the admittedly reprehensible aspects.

An example is his discussion of civil disobedience. He argues thus: "If you accept a democratic system, this means that you are prepared to put up with those of its workings, legislative or administrative, with which you do not agree as well as those that meet with your concurrence. This willingness to accept, in principle, the workings of a system based on the will of the majority, even when you yourself are in the minority, is simply the essence of democracy." Later on, he describes the principle of civil disobedience in these terms: "Some people, who accept our political system, believe that they have a right to disregard it and to violate the laws that have flowed from it so long as they are prepared, as a matter of conscience, to accept the penalties established for such behavior."

To take these points in turn: The essence of democracy is *not* the will of the majority. This is merely the operational basis by which the political machinery of a democracy is allowed to function. The essence of a democracy is, among other things, respect for the rights of minorities and individuals, which in turn implies that the basis of democracy is moral, not operational. This means that there are certain things which a majority cannot do, even if it wished to. What Kennan is describing is "democracy" as defined by Aristotle — namely, mob rule concealed by parliamentary procedure.

The second point, that concerned with breaking the law, is a misstatement of the real intent of civil disobedience. The intent is to call forcibly to attention the possibility that some of those "workings, legislative or administrative," may be overstepping the moral limits. The willingness to suffer the prescribed penalty serves to underscore the intensity and seriousness of feeling: it is not the purpose of civil disobedience. It is true, as Kennan says, that "respect for the law is not an obligation which is exhausted or obliterated by willingness to accept the penalty for breaking it," but, equally, respect for the law also requires the careful scrutiny of specific laws. Admittedly, civil disobedience is an extreme remedy, to be resorted to only when all of the less drastic appeals have been exhausted. Nevertheless, the various court tests of segregation in public facilities, loyalty oaths for teachers, censorship laws, and laws prohibiting the sale and dissemination of birth control devices and information (to give a few examples) would never have come to pass had someone not been willing to violate them and pay the legally prescribed penalty.

Civil disobedience points up the conflict, described by Aristotle, between the good citizen and the good man. The good citizen merely obeys the laws; the good man asks first whether the laws are just. It is distressing to see a man of Kennan's intellectual power descending to such shabby rhetoric — the example of the man who sends in the false fire alarm — in order to discredit a serious moral undertaking.

Sincerely yours,
THOMAS I. DIAMONDSTONE
Assistant Professor of Mathematics
Ohio State University

IV

MR. KENNAN REPLIES

i

When I agreed to say some words at the opening of the new library at Swarthmore College on December 9, 1967, I had no thought of opening a personal polemic with, or about, the radical Left on the American college campus. The occasion was the opening of a new library. I tried to picture this new library in my imagination. In doing so I dredged up from memory certain architects' drawings I had once seen of other new academic libraries: clean, austere, modern structures, with the accent on the horizontal — spacious, sunny terraces — one or two inked-in student figures, laden with books and sauntering, deep in meditation, across the sunny terraces — the whole impregnated with the spirit of serenity and repose. It seemed to me that these drawings reflected the concept of the university as a quiet place, a place of withdrawal and contemplation and learning, that had lain at the foundation of the establishment of so many of our colleges and universities — Swarthmore included, I dare say — and was reflected in their gothic or classical architecture. And I was struck at once by the contrast between this concept of the place of learning and the state of mind, as reflected in appearance, utterance and behavior, of so many of the present inhabitants of these campuses. This contrast, surely, had something important to say to us about the problems of higher education in our country and in our day. It might, therefore, be worth notice, and a bit of comment, on such an occasion.

I proceeded accordingly. To illustrate the earlier ideal of academic detachment I fell back on Woodrow Wilson's words, spoken at the Princeton Sesquicentennial, which I recalled once reading. (I cited them: I did not, as so many students supposed, espouse them.) The opposite pole of outlook and feeling was something I was obliged to evoke out of what I had seen or read of what was going on in the minds of the radical element among the student population. I had no pretensions, and certainly did not mean to assert any, to being an authority on the feelings and reactions of these people. That is not my business. But few of us — and few of us, in particular, who frequent academic campuses in whatever capacity — are permitted to remain entirely oblivious to these things; the students themselves see to that. And on this meager but, I think, not wholly inaccurate fund of impression, I made so bold as to draw.

I came away from the podium, that December afternoon, feeling that I had done my best to speak honestly about matters that might be presumed to be on the minds of other people present. But no sooner had I emerged from the stage door of the College's auditorium than I was made aware — by the presence there of a group of angry young men, mostly bearded, who hissed their disagreement and resentment at me like a flock of truculent village geese — that I had stepped on some tender nerves. And when, some weeks later, the speech was printed in the *New York Times Magazine,* and letters from aroused students and their adult sympathizers began pouring in by the score both to the editor and to myself, it was made quite clear that I had spoken casually about things which it was not to be forgiven to me for speaking about in this manner; that in doing so I had raised more questions than I had answered; and that I was to be held strictly to account.

What I am now writing is, as nearly as I can make it, this accounting. It is not addressed directly to those who wrote the letters. They are too varied in their views for anything of that sort. The great majority were students and teachers, ranging all the way from the most favorable to the most negative — from a lady prepared to support me for the Presidency to the professor of philosophy whose indignation was so great that he called on me to stage a personal breakdown in front of my children (as a gesture of contrition, I gather) and then went on to challenge me publicly to a duel.*

* I do not mean to make light of the proposal that I stage a breakdown before my children. The writer meant it in all seriousness, I am sure, as something to apply symbolically to my entire generation. I include it only to illustrate the violence of negative feeling which my observations aroused in some quarters. I cannot believe, actually, that my own children are so unaware of my own awareness of my faults that they would be greatly enlightened by such a spectacle, however much they might enjoy it for its unexpected dramatic aspects.

137

What I have in mind to do here is simply to comment on some of the implications of this formidable body of literature — letters and published articles together — that the speech unleashed. And the comments are intended for whoever, young or old, cares to read them. If students find in them responses to some of the points they raised in their letters, so much the better.

I should like, however, to reassure the student letter-writers on one point: they have at least been heard. I have read, pondered and made notes on every single one of their letters as well as those of the adults who spoke for them or about them — to a total of over two hundred. I have also read, where I could find it, the published or circulated literature some of them thought I ought to read in order to understand their feelings. To all of them who have said — and this was the keynote of many letters — "Nobody listens to us," I can truthfully say: "I, at least, have listened."

I believe, furthermore, that I got the message. I think I could write a composite letter listing the sources of student discontent and frustration. I know, now, that the state of the American Negro — initially in the South but more recently in the Northern urban ghettos — has troubled their consciences and has caused many of them to feel they must "do something about it." I am aware that what many of them have already done in this respect took great courage and idealism and fortitude of spirit. I know that the students are immensely upset by the combination of Vietnam and the draft: that they view our military effort in Vietnam as a wicked,

138

immoral war against the Vietnamese people; that they feel their own consciences to be engaged in the question as to whether they should permit themselves to be drafted for participation in such a war. I understand that they find this question, notwithstanding the fact that it does not have to be answered until they complete their undergraduate years, to be so harrowing and to harbor such apocalyptic implications that it is silly to suggest they should have their minds primarily on their studies while this looms before them. I further understand that they find intolerable to their sensibilities the fact that industrial firms which supply our armed services, not to mention the Marine Corps itself, should be permitted to recruit on campus; that they see in this, as well as in the fact that universities accept research contracts from the government, evidence that the universities have placed themselves at the service of American "imperialism"; and that they wonder whether they, the students, by consenting even to be students in such places, are not being contaminated with a share of the attendant guilt. I understand that they feel frustrated and desperate because, although they have tried to make their views known, the Administration has showed no signs of paying attention to them. Therefore, they feel, no adequate means of expression are open to them but noise, demonstration, and — some would say — revolution.

I also know that the regular means of political self-expression in such a country as our own, and particularly the electoral channel, seem to these students wholly inadequate; anything of that sort, they consider, would take too long; besides, the country isn't really run by the ostensibly elected government — it is run by something called the "establishment" or the "power structure," to which students have no access and could have no access by honorable means. I understand, finally, that they consider themselves to be adults and therefore entitled to use college property and facilities for whatever purpose suits them — sexual, alcoholic, narcotic, or what you will — without being subjected to a demeaning restriction at the hands of college authorities.

One more thing. May I reiterate that I know myself to be dealing here largely with the left wing of the American student population, and I am aware that this is only a small proportion of the total. I said this in the speech. It was printed in the magazine. But many failed to notice it. If I choose, here again, to deal at such length with this one element, it is because it includes many fine and valuable people, who deserve attention for their own sakes, but also — as I said in the speech — because to some extent the impulses these extremists embody make themselves felt in other segments of the student population as well. It is obvious that students, like Marxists, acutely dislike the feeling of being outflanked to the left. There is always something impressive and disturbing about the fellow who is just a bit more desperate, more flamboyant, more defiant of authority, further out, than yourself. I am speaking here, therefore, not just to the entire intellectual and emotional personality of certain students on the extreme radical fringe, but also to worries, doubts, attractions, and uncertainties that are experienced in one degree or another much further afield.

ii

First, some general observations.

One of the points most often thrown up to me, by faculty members and students alike, in rebuttal to my piece, is that the members of the campus left, far from being poor students, are often the most brilliant and talented and alert of the lot. This is not impossible.* I know many brilliant men who are also very confused. The two qualities do not preclude each other.

One cannot help but note how strongly and unfavorably the use of language by students has been affected by what I think of, and can only describe as, the "social science" style: that learned gobbledygook evolved by their betters on faculties as a means of talking about the nature and activity of human beings in a jargon suggesting

* Here, the evidence seems to be confusing. Mr. Jack New-field, in his anything but unsympathetic study of the New Left (*A Prophetic Minority,* New York: Signet Books, 1966), states (p. 87): "There is an appalling anti-intellectualism among the newer S.D.S. (Students for a Democratic Society) members. Not only do they read few novels and almost no scientific or philosophical literature, they have read little within the radical tradition."

In this respect, I may add, these radical American students differ sharply and unfavorably from the radical Russian students of the Tsarist period whom in other respects they so strongly resemble. These latter read extremely widely in precisely the categories Mr. Newfield mentions.

141

scientific detachment, as though the writer stood on some Archimedian platform outside the boundaries of his own subject matter and was, like the exact scientist, neither here nor there. For an example of the effect on the youth of this persistent attempt to talk about the human predicament in inhuman terms, one has only to consult the document which I suppose is the nearest thing to a programmatical statement of the views of the Students for a Democratic Society: the so-called *Port Huron Statement.* Here we are told, in what appears to be one of many such efforts to express the simple in the most complicated way, that "the political order should serve to clarify problems in a way instrumental to their solution," and that "channels should be commonly available to relate men to knowledge and to power so that private problems from bad recreation facilities to personal alienation are formulated as general issues," etc. In this, as in much of the student writing, we see, I regret to say, the clear influence of a certain contemporary style of faculty writing; and we can realize that in their confusions of mind, if not in other respects, these students are the products of the influence of people older and no less confused than themselves.

A second thing that stands out in these letters is the lack of humor and of any *joie de vivre.* This factor has far more than a casual relationship to the sources of their malaise. When a thoughtful mother, disturbed over the drifting away of her son into the fixations of political extremism, noted in her letter to me that "his other interests and sense of humor have vanished," she was noting a symptom central to the phenomenon that concerned her. The politics, like what one suspects to be the love life of many of these young people, is tense, anxious, defiant and joyless. No wonder their view of the country fills them with desperation. The inability to see and enjoy the element of absurdity in human behavior carries with it the inability to see what is pathetic and appealing and reassuring in what other people do — the inability, also, to detect one's self in the behavior of others. In these circumstances, human forces easily take on a dark, sinister and repellent aspect. One learns to deal with partial manifestations of the individual personality rather than with its human totality — to see people in the impersonal mass rather than as individuals.

I must note, further, that in all these outpourings of personal feeling, many of them related in the most intimate way to the possibilities for satisfaction and self-realization in later life, not once is there the slightest recognition of nature as a possible compensating or sustaining factor in the face of social or political frustration. To none of the student writers does it seem to occur that such frustration might conceivably be alleviated by the enjoyment of nature: by a proximity to animals and wildlife or by an occupation with growing things. I realize, of course, that gardening and all forms of soil-tilling tend generally to be the solace of older people. But this is not true of the wild outdoors. I have the impression that the students who write these protesting letters are almost exclusively people of urban

143

background, that student radicalism, in fact, is primarily an urban phenomenon. If this is true, it is in itself a very interesting fact, and one which might well be taken into account when it comes to the question of how to meet the unrest that drives them.

The counterpart of this lack of interest in nature as a possible sustaining and healing factor in their own lives is an equivalent lack of interest in the protecting and preserving of it. I am struck, as I read these letters, with the fact that whereas my own concern over the course of our American civilization is scarcely less than that of most of the writers, one of the main sources of it is the reckless corruption and destruction of natural environment that our present way of life involves. This is, actually, a process from which they, the younger generation, who are going to have to face the effects thirty or forty years hence, stand much more to suffer than I do. Yet with one very fleeting exception, not a single mention of this occurs in any of the letters. The minds of their authors are absorbed with the problems of man's encounter with man, not with his encounter with nature. And this, too, I fear, increases the difficulty of their problem. For in their preoccupation with man's treatment of man in the social setting, they ignore the possibility that a concerted effort to restore something of the balance and purity and strength of natural environment might be one of the ways in which men could work together without invoking those aspects of political and commercial competition which lead to wars, or

144

fears of wars, and to exploitation, or suspicions of exploitation.

This obliviousness to nature as an object of interest and as a potentially helpful factor in men's lives is connected with another characteristic of this generation of students that is of even broader significance and presents a particularly sharp contrast to the student population of my own day. This is the lack of interest in the creation of any real style and distinction of personal life generally. While this often finds its expression most strikingly in dress, it goes much deeper and enters into manners, tidiness, physical environment and even personal hygiene. The idea that life could be made richer, more tolerable and enjoyable, and even perhaps more useful socially, by an emphasis on the being as well as the doing, by a cultivation of the amenities, by the creation of a dignified and attractive personal environment; the recognition that if great masses of people are to be elevated out of degradation or vulgarity it is important that some people should set an example of graciousness and good taste; the thought that one might even gain strength as an individual and communicate some of it to his intimate entourage by lending to his personal life qualities that sustain confidence in the very possibility of a rich, wholesome and unsordid human experience: all this seems to be quite foreign to the writers of these letters.

Theoretically this is explicable, I suppose, by the fact that — as we shall note shortly — their concerns often relate, most nobly and commendably, to the plight of

145

people other than themselves. But even here (and this is largely a question of the civil rights and anti-poverty movements) one is struck by the absence of any feeling for the power of example. What others are to be emancipated from is reasonably clear. What they are to be emancipated *to* is more puzzling, particularly when the emancipators pursue a mode of life and appearance not noticeably superior to their own.

Another explanation, frequently heard, is that the studied cultivation of ugliness and disorder is a reaction to, and rebellion against, the sterile pretension and conventionalism of the parents' lives. The impression is conveyed of a generation of parents cultivating idle luxury and pretense, disdainfully aloof from the sufferings and problems of the remainder of mankind.

To anyone born before World War I, this explanation has a most curious ring. If anyone had a right to such feelings, it was the student population of my day and earlier ones. *Then,* there really was such a thing as a wealthy "establishment." There was, then, real ostentation, stuffiness, snobbery. What does this generation of students know about these things? What they profess to be rebelling against is only the palest afterglow of what they are talking about. It cannot really be a parental style of life they are opposing, because this scarcely exists. If an arrogant, stuffy "power structure," composed of people cultivating a spiritually shallow, selfish and extravagant mode of life for their own personal satisfaction, is really necessary to the members of this student generation as a foil to their own inner need for re-

146

bellion and self-assertion, then they are going to have to create it themselves. The belief that it exists in the person of their unfortunate parents — servantless, hounded by the tax collector, enchained to the suburban automobile, the filling station and the supermarket — is a figment of their imagination.

I would like to note, finally, the shrill indignation that runs through most of these letters over the suggestion that students might, while at college, do well to have their minds rather on their studies than on contemporary political affairs. The terms in which I am put in my place for this suggestion, both by letter-writers and by students I have talked to, run the full range of rejection from scorn to pity. This, I am told, is just silly; the idea of noninvolvement is foreign to the spirit and atmosphere of the present campus; the very utterance of such a thought shows that I understand nothing of the present-day student and his problems.

Very well; so be it. I shall examine, a bit further on, some of the reasons for this feeling. What I was concerned to point out in the article, and what I would like now to emphasize once more, is the conflict that exists between this outlook and the academic tradition that inspired the establishment and development of a great many of our centers of learning.

I don't mean to say that a passionate involvement in contemporary affairs is necessarily reprehensible. As an extreme, it is probably preferable to its opposite, which would be a total indifference to public problems. But it does suggest a conflict of some seriousness. If one were

147

replying individually to many of these letters, one would feel like saying: "Very well. We understand the passionate quality of your interest in contemporary affairs — the depth of your concern, the agony of your conscience. We accept your statement that you have learned more from one thing or another that you have done by way of participation in the excitements of the present political scene — demonstrations, work in the ghettos and whatnot — than from all your professors and textbooks. We agree that this is all very selfless, very high-minded, very courageous. But what in the hell — if we might be so bold as to ask — are you doing on a university campus?"

I come away from the reading of these letters with the feeling that if we are going to insist that young people spend four years at this particular stage of life in some place having nominally to do with education, then we need two kinds of universities. One, designed presumably for the majority, would consist of institutions devoted to what I might call the breathless and backgroundless preoccupation with, and action upon, the passing scene. Its curriculum would be one uninterrupted current affairs course, consisting primarily of off-campus field work, participation in demonstrations, social work, political organizational activity, etc., punctuated occasionally by reading periods devoted to the pages of daily newspapers and weekly news magazines and to seminars on the burning problems of the day and the techniques of mass political action. Attention of both students and professors would drift collectively, here, with the excitements of the time; it would be frowned upon, as in Russia, to go to the library and ask to see the pages of a newspaper more than five years old; and the student would be prepared to take his place, as a member of the crowd, in the uncritical pursuit of various mass-emotional causes.

But side by side with these places (though not too close to them) I think we ought perhaps also to have a few institutions of another sort — humble, inconspicuous, unassuming ones — for the instruction of that smattering of young people who might be curious about life in its wider and more permanent aspects and might want to take these particular years of their life to tap something of the accumulated wisdom of the ages about the nature of man and his predicament. These could be regarded, if you will, as queer ones, as oddities of our civilization, like devotees of various curious hobbies; but they should not be disturbed in their pursuits.

I am serious about this. If the respect for intellectual detachment, and for learning in the true sense, is really as small as it would seem to be from these letters and from other students' reactions, then the contemporary campus is no place for the odd man who might like to devote himself to the acquisition and furtherance of knowledge. Conversely, if an educational establishment is going to cling to the theory that it is a place for the calm study of man and nature and thought, then it is no place for the student whose general interest and concern is for the contribution he can make now, right away, while a student, to public causes beyond the campus.

In attempting to understand the unhappiness of these young people, it might be well to start with the ostensible objects of their concern. Leaving aside for a moment the draft, these are outstandingly three: the state of the American Negro and the underprivileged generally; Vietnam; and the disciplinary constraints of the college campus.

In its involvement with the civil rights movement in the South, and with efforts to relieve the plight of the Negro in the large urban centers, the radical student Left is following a course that has strong parallels with that of the young Russian Populists of the 1860's and '70's. As in the case of these latter, it is not their own plight these people are concerned to alleviate. All evidence suggests that they are largely the children of middle-class, even upper-middle-class, families. Neither they nor their families have suffered inordinately, as a rule, from poverty, lack of status, or lack of civil rights. (The fact that they have not done so is, incidentally, something they take entirely for granted, and for which they experience no sense of appreciation. They are mindful only of the problems their society has *not* solved, not of the ones it has.) Their grievance against American society is not that it has mistreated *them* but that it has not treated others equally well. And so, like their Russian forebears, the object of whose indignation was the treatment of a Russian peasantry to which they did not belong and of which they had little real knowledge, these American idealists "go to the people," in the sense of the Negro community, endeavoring not only to bring them enlightenment and comfort but to support them in movements of protest for which, in some instances, the people concerned have little interest or stomach. And like these Russian counterparts, once again, they often get small thanks for their pains, finding themselves misunderstood, rejected and mistreated by the very people they are attempting to help.*

One wonders about the reasons for this. The phenomenon of concern by intellectuals for miseries they do not share but which they take as offenses to their conscience is of course a familiar one in the history of Western civilization. Hardship and injustice are real phenomena; but revolutionary protest against such things is usually the product of stimulus from outsiders with a comfortable background. By and large, that is the history of the entire Marxist-socialist movement.

Yet this impulse to defend not one's own interests but those of others is not experienced — or at least not in the same degree — by every generation of student youth. In Russia, Kropotkin's generation experienced it; Pushkin's generation, by and large, had not; and this — although the situation of the peasantry was in many respects worse in Pushkin's time than it was in the 1870's. Similarly in this country: my generation of students —

* In his treatise on the radical student Left, referred to above, Mr. Jack Newfield states, in relation to the work in the ghettos, that "many project workers have been beaten up, and a few of the girls have been almost raped. Almost all the projects have been robbed repeatedly" (p. 102).

151

that of the 1920's — felt no need to exert itself on behalf of the Southern Negro or the urban poor (of whom even at that time there was no lack). Why the difference?

It would be easy to reply that this present generation is a particularly wonderful one — idealistic and courageous in a degree we were not. Perhaps. But then, why? Whole generations are not born one way or another just by accident. Does the answer really lie just in this — in the obvious misery and degradation of the objects of their attention? Or does it represent the expression of some inner need, to which the objects have only a casual relevance? If these particular objects of concern, compassion and indignation did not exist, would the students search for others?

Proof is lacking; the question is hypothetical. But it seems to me that the presumption lies with an affirmative answer. The speed with which the focus of student concern has switched from the Negro of the rural South to the Negro of the urban North, and then to Vietnam, and then to the disciplinary regime of the college campus, suggests strongly to me that the real seat of discomfort lies not in the objects that attract these feelings but in some inner distress and discontent with contemporary society that would find other issues to fasten to as points of grievance against the established order, even if the present ones did not exist.

It is worth examining in somewhat greater detail the view of the Negro problem that emerges from much of the literature of the New Left.

First of all, the students tend to attribute the Negro's plight, whether in the South or in the Northern urban ghetto, exclusively to the cruelty and indifference of the white community now alive. No account is taken of the complex and stubborn historical roots of this problem. In the case of the South, custom, culture and inheritance are less than dismissed: they are not even noted. In the case of the Northern ghettos, there is no trace of a recognition of the fact that cities in question did not invite the enormous influx of Negro residents that has occurred in recent decades; that they were not prepared for it and could scarcely have been expected to be; that it is not easy for any community to absorb into its life in a short space of time great masses of people of a cultural background different from that of its regular inhabitants; that all this takes time and patience.

Nor is there any evidence of a recognition that the Negro has had any part in the creation of his own problem, or is to have any part in its solution. The idea that he could improve his situation in any degree, either by his own effort or by his electoral action, appears to be strange to this cast of thought. He is seen only as the helpless ward of public authority. One gains from the reading of these letters the impression that in the view of their writers, the American Negro is to be held to no standards — that all qualities on his part, whether laziness, dishonesty, irresponsibility and violence of behavior or their opposites, are to be rewarded alike.

In entertaining this view, the students are only reflecting, of course, the prevailing climate of American

153

opinion with relation to social problems — a climate in which such terms as thrift, honesty and industry (in the personal sense) have disappeared from the vocabulary, and the discussion of the emoluments people might properly receive is never — but really never — connected in any way with the measure of initiative, integrity, and hard work they are prepared to put forth. And in defense of such an outlook the students would point, of course, to the handicaps the Negro labors under: to the continued denial of civil rights in many parts of the South, to the inferior educational facilities available to him there and elsewhere, to the limitations on housing and employment existing in a great many communities.

In all of this, they would be right insofar as these conditions really prevail — but only so far. Yet their letters show no evidence of a willingness to consider any such gradations. The pattern is wholly without shading. Such progress as *has* been made in the treatment of the American Negro gets as short shrift from them as it does from the Negro leaders. To read these letters, no one would ever dream that there were any American Negroes who *did* enjoy civil rights, who *did* attend school with white children, who *did* receive higher education or advance in business, government, and the professions. The whole great fund of good will and helpfulness that has been forthcoming from parts of the white community disappears completely from this picture, as does every suggestion of a responsibility on the side of the Negro himself; and the image is left only of a cold, heartless, cruel white society, encumbered with total guilt and total power, facing a Negro population marked only by helplessness, innocence, and nobility of spirit.

I say these things with great reluctance, because I know they will be distorted and interpreted as evidence of an outlook I do not really entertain. I yield to none in my admiration for many of the qualities I see in the American Negro. Aside from the distinction of his contributions to music and the drama and humor, he has an exceptionally high sensitivity to people and situations. He has a gift for casual social intercourse that many of us could envy, and one made all the more impressive by the respect and solicitude for the dignity of the other person that underlie it. When not upset by painful racial reactions or demoralized by the various strains and artificialities of urban life, he tends, accordingly, to have better natural manners than a great many American whites. To anyone who believes, as I do, in the overriding importance of good form as an essential of civilized living, these are formidable qualities; and our country, in my opinion, would be distinctly poorer without them. I am perfectly willing, furthermore, to recognize that the responsibility for the present situation of the American Negro is considerably greater on the part of the white community than it is on his.

But the simplistic character of the view of the Negro problem that comes through in these letters alarms me, because it bodes no good for the future. The frustration these students are now experiencing in the face of this problem is not going to be relieved in the manner they are demanding. The American Negro is not going to be aided by an approach which treats him only as object and not at all as subject. Nor will the nature of the problem itself ever be understood from an approach that treats it so extensively as a moral one. Of course, the instances of individual injustice, heartlessness and brutality have been legion, and each in itself inexcusable. But when great masses of people react in the same way, as masses of American whites have done in their confrontation with this problem, the serious student must put moral judgment aside and search for deeper, more elementary, and less conscious causes. Either the radical student view of this problem mellows and matures, or the frustration that now eats on its bearers and poisons their relation to their own national society is bound to increase.

A similar impression is conveyed by their view of Vietnam.* For those who may not know it (numbers of people appear not to; several even wrote me that instead of criticizing the students I should get out and oppose the war), I was long an opponent of the policies that brought us to the Vietnam involvement; I made my views public on a number of occasions in ways (including five hours on national TV on one occasion alone) that could scarcely have been more emphatic without defeating their own effectiveness. I continue to regard the war as one devoid of favorable prospects, highly dangerous to world peace, and dreadfully adverse in its ef-

* My argument and the letters were, of course, written before President Johnson's announcement of the partial bombing pause in Vietnam and are to be considered apart from it.

fects on our domestic life and world position. Having said this, I trust I shall not be misunderstood when I say that the view of the Vietnam conflict that emerges from these letters is grotesquely overdrawn. Again, the unsuspecting reader would come away with the impression that we had deliberately and gratuitously attacked Vietnam — both North and South — with a view to subjecting it to some sort of permanent American colonial domination, and that we are behaving there with the most callous and deliberate cruelty, lining people up before the firing squads or dropping napalm on them out of no other motive than an imperialistic determination to subjugate them to our political will.

Sickening as are the civilian casualties we have had a part in producing, and strongly as I myself deplore and disapprove the actions that have occasioned them, I have to point out that this is, again, a dangerously oversimplified view of a complex situation. That there can indeed be instances where the seizure of power by a Communist minority in another country harbors dangers and disadvantages that are properly the concern of American statesmanship; that the opponent we face in Vietnam yields to none in brutality; that much of the suffering brought to civilians has been deliberately provoked by this opponent; that the alternative to our effort there would be the subjection of the South Vietnamese people to a dictatorship far more ruthless, bloody and vindictive than any regime we have been trying — in our fumbling, unsuccessful way — to assure to them; that the process of disengagement from Vietnam would

157

in any case have to be a gradual and delicately guided one if serious damage were not to be done both to the political stability of the Southeast Asian region and to our own record for reliability and fidelity to engagements in international affairs; and that the totality of our action in Vietnam might well classify as a massive imprudence but scarcely as a deliberate crime: — none of this is visible in the student view of this conflict. It is an immoral war; we have all decided that it is; it would be shocking to question the proposition; and *basta*.

Where, one wonders, have the teachers been while a view so lacking in balance and in historical perspective was being formed? If one of the purposes of college education is to enable people to look at public affairs in all their true complexity and to place them in some sort of historical perspective, then there has been something very wrong, at some point, with much of the teaching of history and politics in this country.

I wonder how many of these students have taken account of the implications of the view they profess to entertain of the motives of American statesmanship in the Vietnam conflict. It is a view that is, unfortunately, almost identical with that which Communist propagandists have been endeavoring, for a full half-century, to communicate to the world public. We have now played extensively into the hands of these propagandists; and it is no exaggeration to say that today hundreds of millions of people outside our borders have become convinced, or semi-convinced, that our motives are little different from those of Hitler. Were this really true, then the demand of any right-thinking person would have to be not just that we "get out of Vietnam" but indeed that we withdraw entirely from any and all active participation in world affairs, for surely there could be no other involvement on our part, military or nonmilitary, that would not be corrupted by such a pattern of motivation. A government so motivated could not be trusted to conduct constructively any active policy in international life. This is already the way we are regarded by a great many people; and so appalling is the resulting effect on the interpretation of our actions that I personally think it will take years of forbearance and noninvolvement — years of a semi-isolationism — to eradicate the suspicions of our motives that have already become ingrained in large sections of the world public. But how many of the students have thought this through, and whether they recognize this isolationism as the logical implication of their own outlook, is something one must be permitted to doubt. Most of them do not, after all, consider themselves isolationists.

iv

Intimately connected with the problem of Vietnam, and constituting by far the most acute single source of student unrest, not just for the extensively alienated students of the radical Left but the larger part of the male student body in general (and, by infection, for some of the female part as well), is the draft. Its role in this respect is quite central. It affects and exacerbates many of the other sources of discontent and of bizarre or destructive behavior. It multiplies enormously the intensity of feeling over Vietnam, insofar as it causes the students to feel they are being compelled to accept some degree of complicity and moral responsibility for our part in the war. It is offered by students as the first and most unassailable reason why they are unable, during their undergraduate years, to concentrate on their studies and to let their engagement in current political affairs hold over to a later stage in their lives. Much of the frantic, compulsive character of their indulgence in the fields of sex and narcotics, as well as in various forms of political extremism, are rationalized on the grounds that "tomorrow we die." Their relationship to the existing political system of the country is deeply affected by the reflection that they have to be twenty-one before they can vote, whereas the government, in the form of the draft board, can theoretically lay hands on them at the age of eighteen, thus inflicting upon them a hardship with relation to which they themselves have had nothing to say.

And finally, because resentment of the draft, and fear of it, reaches so wide a spectrum of the student body, it greatly enhances the influence of the radical Left on campus; for the extremists, who are the first and loudest in their protests, have here an issue on which the others can be easily reached. The leaders of the student Left stand as teachers to the rest in the new science of draft evasion — a science which, sometimes with the encouragement and participation of faculty members, is rapidly becoming a popular course of instruction, with its own devotees, classes, seminars, textbook literature, experts, and even faculty. It is not an exaggeration to say that an abandonment of the draft would alone cure a large part of the troubles of the present generation of students: both those of which they themselves are conscious and those that impinge themselves, as disturbing features of student behavior, on the consciousness of older people.

Here again, let us note certain specific aspects of this student reaction. First of all: the violent resentment of the draft appears to be unmodified by the slightest trace of any sense of obligation to country or pride in the wearing of the uniform of the armed services of the United States. What in earlier decades would have carried with it at least the suspicion of cowardice or lack of patriotism is today pursued wholly without shame or hesitation. It is, in fact, elevated to the status of a positive virtue. It is the smart chap, the skillful and intelligent one, the one to be admired, who successfully evades the draft.

I wonder whether this attitude is not in part a predictable reaction to the silly cultivation of the externals of an exaggerated hurrah-patriotism that has come over our schools in the past twenty years: the oaths and songs and flaggings and renderings of the National Anthem on any and all occasions. These things are, unless I am much mistaken, relics of the anti-Communist hysteria of the late 1940's and early 1950's, when the pious and frequent performance of such ritualistic manifestations of love of country became a means of self-defense before the aroused bodies of super-patriots who swept through libraries, schools and colleges, their nostrils quivering for the smell of Communist treason. Many of the students would say, of course, that it is not the country itself but the "establishment" they are rebelling against — not the nation but the reactionary and oppressive policies to which the nation has allowed itself to be committed — that what they are doing reflects not lack of any love of country but rather a shame of country which the very love for it has induced. And in this there would be much truth.

We must note, furthermore, that this attitude is not universal among the students, nor is it always unmixed with contradictory impulses. Many students go cheerfully to their military service. Many others evade it only with the heaviest sense of unhappiness.

The fact remains that the present student attitude toward obligations of military service stands in stark and almost dangerous contrast to concepts that prevailed up until quite recently among the majority of our people. To many older people it is almost bound to appear as a provocation offered to some of their most deeply held feelings. Many will question whether the emergence in so short a time of so drastically altered a concept of the relation of the individual to the state does not spell a fundamental change in the very nature of American national feeling.

But here, too, one must note the strong streak of hysteria and exaggeration that pervades the student view. With all due concern for, and horror over, the casualties that the Vietnam conflict has occasioned (already exceeding those of the American forces involved in the Normandy invasion), the fact remains that not every young American who leaves college is drafted, nor is every one who is drafted assigned to a combat unit, nor is every one assigned to a combat unit sent to Vietnam, nor do all those sent to Vietnam see combat, nor are all those who do see combat killed or wounded, nor — for that matter — is it at all certain that when the time comes for many of those now in college to graduate the Vietnam conflict will still be actively in progress. Exact comparative figures are hard to come by, but I would think it likely that the actuarial chances of a college student living to the age of forty at the time when I was a boy, in the face of the uncontrollability of infectious diseases in that day, were smaller than those same chances as they relate to the average college student today, even including the hazards of Vietnam.* (This, incidentally, did not prevent either the college campuses of that time, or the bohemian-intellectual colonies in the great cities, from being the scenes of a great deal of gaiety, good spirit, confidence and love of life.)

Yet to read many of the student letters or indeed

* I am reliably informed that the probability of a recent male college graduate being drafted and killed in action was 10 per 100,000 in 1966, and 30 per 100,000 in 1967. That this will rise in 1968 is to be expected, if deplored. It would have to rise very materially before the risk would become a substantial one. Even the figure for 1967 is less than half the death rate in motor vehicle accidents for those from fifteen to twenty-four years of age, which is 69.6 per 100,000.

163

much of the college literature relating to the draft one could only conclude that every male college student of this day faced, upon leaving college, either certain death or a rotting away in the country's prisons. The letters abound with such suggestions. "The unworldly, gawky, senior, English major," writes a young man from Cambridge, Massachusetts, who presumably himself corresponds to this description,

. . . who has lost his deferment and does not want to fight in a war he hardly understands but can see is meaningless and evil, . . . awakened to the horrors in which he will be ordered to participate, confronted with the unreasonable, unreasoned, unjustifiable murders he will be forced to commit, has time only to scream his protest, to block a Dow recruiter, to refuse to step forward before his personal and moral anguish are silenced by prison walls.

"Who can blame them," asks a young man from Philadelphia,

. . . when all that awaits them on graduation is a letter from the President, a free trip to Vietnam and a trip home in a green plastic bag?

So gloomily histrionic, in fact, is the view of the draft that flows from these communications that I was almost heartened to find among the letters one from a young man who saw me as a "bleeding-heart and father figure," and could think of no other message that "might get through" to me than the reminder, "Oh Dad, poor

Dad, we'll be around long after you are dead and gone."
Here was at least one who evidently expected to survive Vietnam.

One must doubt that these somewhat dramatic protests really reflect the sober thoughts of the letter-writers. Most of these latter, I suspect, know pretty well what the real actuarial prospects are for personal disaster as a result of the draft, and few of them, if any, are lacking in courage. What they cannot stand, however, and what the government seems determined to inflict upon them in maximum degree, is uncertainty. They want, anxiously and desperately, far more than was the case with those of us who graduated from college in the 1920's, to be able to foresee their future life and to plan it. They are the victims of that preoccupation with personal security which, curiously, is more pronounced in this age of social security systems, medicare, and elaborate pension arrangements, when security is abundantly available, than was the case fifty years ago, when there was little of it at all in the formal sense. For this reason, the draft, with all its vagaries and uncertainties, making havoc as it does of any and all attempts to plan intelligently ahead for the years following graduation, produces on students an effect much more disturbing, frustrating and demoralizing than would have been the case in an earlier day, when the external foundations of personal security were smaller, and the internal sources far greater, than is now the case.

While we are on the subject of the draft, I may as well digress a moment to mention that point in my article on which I was most widely, and in part justly, criticized: namely, the subject of civil disobedience. I am free to admit that I dealt with this subject, as Mr. Auden and others pointed out, much too cavalierly.

I was struck with the statement, in a letter from another of my correspondents, Mrs. Rosalind Marimont of Wheaton, Maryland, that she was unable to arrive at any satisfactory general answer to this problem, and found herself obliged to fall back "on the unsatisfying answer that each case must be decided on its merits."

I am sure she is right. It is evident that there could conceivably be, and at times have been, things which public authority has required people to do which no one could, in good conscience, permit to be required of him. Likewise, there could be things, as Mr. Auden suggests, that a person might be required to omit where the requirement would constitute an intolerable invasion of his personal dignity. I recognize that there could be times and occasions, even for the citizen who lives under a system of representative government, when the denial of obedience would be justifiable.

But I should think — and it was this that I meant to emphasize in my speech — that the dimensions of this problem are not quite the same where the citizen has a part in determining public policy — where the social contract may be said to prevail — as they are where the feelings of the citizen are in no wise consulted in determining the policies of the state. For a Gandhi or a Tolstoy civil disobedience was one thing; for a Thoreau — another. It seems to me that the citizen who lives under a system that assures him not only voting rights but extensive guarantees for the inviolability of his person and property, and who accepts the protection of the state in the enjoyment of these rights, owes to the state at least a high measure of respect and forbearance in those instances where he may not find himself in agreement with its policies.

There is obviously a distinction to be made here between defiance by a citizen of an effort on the part of the state to make him perform specific individual actions repugnant to his own conscience and moral feeling, on the one hand, and lawlessness performed by way of protest against general laws or actions of the state conceived by the individual to be unjust, on the other. It is one thing to decline to serve on a firing squad or to destroy villages in which noncombatants are known to be present; it is another thing to obstruct or foul public premises, to hinder others in the performance of their normal professional functions, and then to defy the police action one has one's self provoked — all simply to force a change in public policy.

The burning of a draft card strikes me as an extravagant and indefensible act. It constitutes the defiance of a legal requirement of government at a stage when the specific meaning of that requirement has as yet not been made clear. In this way it becomes a symbol, needlessly flamboyant, needlessly offensive and provocative to other citizens, of the denial of the very obligation of respect for the law generally, not to mention the obligation of loyalty to country. The draft card is not in itself proof that the government has required, or is necessarily going to require, any specific action of its possessor that could normally be held to be offensive to the conscience. The holder of the card could, for all he knows, not be called up at all, or his service could take any one of a hundred forms other than ones involving killing or brutality. To stage the act of defiance and disobedience at this initial point is to deny, by implication, the obligation to take any part in the defense of the country under any circumstances. The policies under which this defense is at the moment being conducted may be ones that the draftee does not like; but they are not ones that he is fully competent to judge, particularly at his age and against the background of his experience. Nor can he know whether they will still be the prevailing policies when and if his obligation of service becomes an active reality. They are in any case not his responsibility. If he has faith in the general soundness of the political system, he must be prepared, as I have said, to accept its workings — even those he doesn't like. If he does not accept its general soundness, if his view of it is not on balance affirmative, he should not himself accept its benefits and its protection. I say "on balance" because it is the citizen's duty, surely, in thinking about his obligations to country, to reflect not just on the country's failures but also on its successes, not just on its errors but also on its

168

achievements, not just on the problems it has failed to solve but also on those with which it has, after all, coped successfully. Whoever does this will find himself obliged to concede to his government a certain margin of error, stupidity and incompetence, within which he still ought to give it whatever help he can.

In arriving at these views I am affected, I must admit, by an inability to follow the logic of pacifism and nonviolence as the bases for a political philosophy. The central function of government, as I see it, is the assurance of the public order. This is something for which nobody has ever found any suitable means that do not include, at some point, the devices of coercion. This is true of the democracy as it is of the dictatorship. Whoever relies on these devices — on the police and the courts and the prisons — as instruments for the assurance of his own protection and his own enjoyment of civil rights — has no moral basis, as I see it, for denying his contribution to their maintenance.

The same applies to the arrangements for the national defense. No one has a moral right to deny on principle his contribution to this part of our national life unless he is willing to condemn not just the war his government is at the moment conducting, but every one that it has conducted in the past, including that which established its political independence; and unless he is really prepared to commit its destinies to the good graces of an extremely jealous and largely hostile outside world. If all were to do this, there would of course then be nothing to prevent the seizure of the reins of government in this country, entirely or in part, by any foreign political entity that wished to seize them and could accommodate its action to the interests of other foreign governments. Our own government would have no means with which to prevent it. But there could be very few forms of foreign rule under which the provocation to civil disobedience would not be far greater, and the punishment of it far more severe, than is the case in our bumbling, confused, in some ways seriously misguided, but relatively tolerant, democracy. The final upshot of such conduct might therefore be expected to be an increase, rather than a decrease, in the total level of brutality and violence. Thus the principle of nonviolence has, when carried to its logical conclusion, a certain self-defeating quality which could give it attraction, it seems to me, only in the eyes of those to whom *le mieux* is always preferable to its well-known enemy, *le bien*.

In the final analysis, the question of civil disobedience is, I am sure, a matter of temperament. Humanity divides, it has been said, between those who, in their political philosophy, place the emphasis on order and those who place it on justice. I belong in the first of those categories. Human justice is always imperfect. The laws on which it bases itself are always to some extent unjust. These laws have therefore only a relative value; and it is only relative benefits that can be expected from the effort to improve them. But the good order of society is something tangible and solid. There is little that can be done about men's motives; but if men can be restrained in their behavior, something is accomplished. To keep

170

them from destroying each other physically on the streets; to commit them to the observance of a minimum of the amenities; to oblige them to observe greater outward decency than is really present in the primitive chaos of their souls — this is in itself an achievement. The benefit of the doubt should lie, therefore, with the forces of order, not with the world-improvers. The process of the maintenance of order inevitably attracts to its performance a certain amount of natural inequity and brutality and even stupidity. There are people who exercise the office of jailer out of a sense of compassion and responsibility toward people less fortunate than themselves; but there are more, I fear, who do it because they enjoy the smell of power or are wholly unimaginative. It cannot be otherwise. This is a sad necessity of the human predicament — a prudent concession to human weakness. And because this is so, a measure of tolerance and acceptance of these things is incumbent on the citizen who looks to the good order of society for his own protection; and this obligation carries even to the point where this citizen finds himself submitting to, perhaps even contributing to, the promulgation of policies he intensely dislikes.

vi

Scarcely less violent than the draft itself, as a factor in student unrest, are the various forms of collaboration, or even mere contact, between the university and the government; particularly, of course, the recruiting

171

on campus by the armed services and by industrial firms who act as suppliers to the American defense forces, but also almost any form of research activity conducted in the universities under governmental contract. Fully as often as the draft itself, in fact, are these arrangements cited in the letters as reasons why there can be no peace and quiet on campus, why it is impossible for the student to concentrate on his studies, why it is impossible for him not to be interested primarily in contemporary causes. These arrangements, but particularly the visible evidences of them on campus, are solemnly accepted as obvious affronts to the feelings of the student; as something he could not reasonably be expected to contemplate with composure; as a symbol, intolerable to his sensibilities, of the unreasonable demands his government places on his person and his conscience.

All this is reflected time and again in the letters.

"The sanctuary of our schools," writes a lady in New York,

where learning requires seclusion and concentration, has been disturbed by the invasion of war-related personnel whose presence reminds [the students] they may soon become educated corpses.

Universities, writes a Columbia student, are becoming increasingly "service stations for military and corporate interests." The mere act of studying in such a place is, whether or not the student is conscious of the fact, an "interest-laden" course of action, "beneficial to an oppressive status quo."

172

A professor of history at a New York community college notes that I (whom he sees as a "hypocrite and a moral disaster") have had the temerity to urge dispassionate inquiry and scholarly seclusion from current affairs. How can I imagine this to be possible, he asks, dramatically,

. . . when at a typical large university one finds the Marines recruiting across the street from the library or in the student lounge, the CIA training or developing programs for counterinsurgency activities in, let us say, the new behavioral sciences complex, research manipulated in almost every area to serve our empire, and the draft used as a club to "channel" the educational and career choices of male students?

Or again, according to Mr. Franz L. Alt, it is the university that has betrayed the scholarly ideal; to the students "the inflammatory spectacle of the University sponsoring on campus the recruiting activities of agents from the CIA, the armed services, manufacturers of napalm, and the like, is intolerable." *

This view is all the more remarkable for the fact that none of the arrangements in question are, so far as I am aware, ones that involve any responsibility or obligation on the part of the student himself. Whether anyone else may some day be held to account for the fact that such arrangements were established and maintained, it is certain that he, the student, cannot and will not be.

* Mr. Alt attributes this last statement to another scholar, whom he does not identify.

173

These arrangements involve no violence to his person or his privacy. No one forces him to talk with the Marine recruiter. The recruiter does not seek him out. He is not, as one might infer from the tone of many of the letters, dragged kicking and screaming to the recruiting tent. No one obliges him to seek service with the Dow Chemical Company or even to discuss such a possibility with the company's representative. When the question is asked, as it was in one of the passages just cited, as to how a student could possibly devote himself to scholarly inquiry when the Marines are recruiting across the street, I am tempted to suggest that the answer is not really all that complicated: this might conceivably be done by the simple expedient of taking a book, going into the library, and reading. I doubt that the recruiter would follow him there. That this is regarded as impossible — that it should be considered as by all means essential that the recruiter be expelled from campus before the student can have peace of mind — and that this, the silencing of a voice that is not even raised except where individually requested, should be demanded by those very students and faculty members who would be most vehement in their insistence that the halls of the university should be thrown open on any and all occasions for public addresses by people who urge the violent overthrow of the existing political order: all this does seem to me to be in part the reflection of a real hysteria, but in part, too, the workings of a curious and widespread confusion concerning the distribution of function and responsibility in our society — a confusion

174

which we shall have to note in greater detail when we turn, as we must presently do, to the political implications of radical student attitudes.

vii

One ought not, I suppose, to leave the discussion of the objects of student unrest without at least mentioning the resentment of parietal rules and the demands raised by students for a larger voice in university administration. These did not figure prominently in the letters addressed to the editor or myself, presumably because I had not mentioned them in the article.* But they are a phenomenon known to exist in one degree or another at most colleges, and particularly among the radical students.

So far as the parietal rules are concerned, what first strikes the attention is the fact that all this anguish over them comes at a time when they have never — across the board — been laxer, more perfunctory, less onerous. What the students are protesting, here, is no more than a final minimal residue of an eroded disciplinary code that once existed in a far more elaborate form. Within this looser, scarcely perceptible framework a thousand

---

* It is significant that this is one of the places where student unrest seems to enjoy some faculty sympathy. "Mr. Kennan," said one professorial colleague, accusingly and triumphantly, "has not faced clearly in himself how he would feel if he were in a room with someone he cared about a great deal and was required to keep the door open." To this reproach I freely confess myself devoid of any adequate answer.

175

forms of self-indulgence are now permitted which in an earlier day would not have been tolerated. Yet one does not recall that this stricter code was a source of discomfort or indignation to the student population of the time. There was amusement over the unavoidable artificiality and absurdity of rules of this nature. There was the usual enjoyment to be derived from trying to break them with impunity. But there was no bitterness. So conspicuous is this anomaly that one is forced to ask oneself whether the real reason for the present mood of protest is not that the rules have been relaxed too much, rather than that they have been relaxed too little.

What students are rebelling against, here, is not really the parietal rules but the residential university or college itself. An institution of this nature cannot get along without such rules. Its very quality as owner and proprietor of property used for residential purposes leaves it no choice but to lay down certain minimal norms for the manner in which that use can proceed. This would be true even if the inhabitants were older people. The trouble with most of the rebellious students, one suspects, is that they don't belong in such a place at all. Their presence there is obviously the result of some sort of misunderstanding. What they want, when they emerge from the classroom, is not the enjoyment of the company of other students (particularly ones of their own sex), and of faculty members, in a residential community. Their compulsive desire to get away from the campus on weekends; their demand for the private automobile as a means of escape; their complaints about the isolation of the campus from large urban centers (even Bryn Mawr, a young lady told me, was too "isolated"); and the unsocial privatism of much of their recreational activity while on campus: all these testify to a disregard and dislike for the very idea of the residential college, a slighting of its potential values, and a chafing, natural enough in the circumstances, over the minimal restraints it implies. Seeing the reaction of students to the residential campus today, one is seized with a feeling of pity for the well-meaning people of earlier decades who endowed these lovely places, and of the taxpayers and alumni contributors who now support them; for the fruits of their generosity are so largely unwanted. They could have saved their money, their good will, and their pains. What a large proportion of students appear now to want is the big-city university on the European pattern, where the administration could not care less where or how they lived, and where, once liberated from the lecture room, they could indulge to their hearts' content the desire to lead what they consider to be an adult life.

The university administration has a certain share of the blame for this state of affairs. In many instances, it has itself impaired the residential quality of the campus by overexpansion; by stretching out the campus itself to a point where it becomes dependent on the automobile for internal communication; by forcing faculty to live miles away from the students; by crowding students into the dormitories to a point where all comfort and privacy are lost; by replacing attractive dining halls with noisy, sloppy cafeterias with turnpike-restaurant food; by forgetting, in short, that there is a critical maximum to the size and density of the residential scholarly community. In this way it has hollowed its own pretenses and made a caricature of its own function.

Whether, had it behaved otherwise, the student would have responded, or to what extent he would have responded, is another question. To be successfully faithful to its own purpose, the residential campus would have to have some of the qualities of a home. But it takes two to make a sense of home — the home and its occupant; and one wonders, in many instances, whether the student of this day would know how to respond to such a place even if it existed. Too often, the childhood house from which he came, its privacy shattered by the squawking tyranny of the TV box, its cohesion destroyed by the social fragmentation of the family into age groups, was itself only the caricature of a home.

It will be said in defense of the university administration that if it has itself impaired the residential quality of the institution, it has done so in order to hold down expenses and to make the place available to a wider, and less affluent, segment of student youth. In the large, publicly supported state and urban universities it is hard to see how this can be avoided; and for the student whose reasons for going to college are purely professional or whose interests and capacity for curiosity are absorbed by the contemporary scene it perhaps makes little difference. But I would like to plead most earnestly for the retention, as perhaps a minor companion

178

piece to these great urban degree factories, of the purely and unabashedly residential small college. There must, after all, be *some* students interested in the pursuit and cultivation of knowledge for its own sake — and a need, accordingly, for surroundings conducive to this process. Such institutions will be expensive — yes. Not everyone will be able to afford to attend them. But there ought also, perhaps, to be some opportunity left to the parent who is prepared to work and save and sacrifice to give his child a superior education. What is important, and what is not always done today, is that there be warned away from such institutions students who do not want or appreciate the amenities of the residential college and are going to resent them if confronted with them.

This is, admittedly, a form of elitism I am talking about, but a voluntary one. Unless this kind of institution is preserved, there is a real possibility, it seems to me, that we may well soon find ourselves faced with a situation in which literally no one in this country can receive a really superior education in the sense of a rich, fruitful and pleasant experience in a true scholarly community.

As for the demand of students for a part in university administration: this is of course a periodic phenomenon of student life in all times and at all places. But as it appears in this country today it is also a reflection of an extreme confusion of mind about all distinctions of function, responsibility and authority, as well as about the meaning of the term "democracy" and its proper

179

applications. This is a confusion sown and multiplied by our public school system, with its tendency to deny both the authority and the responsibility of the teacher, its Pollyannish patter about "good citizenship," its attempt to persuade the little child that he should organize and vote and decide like an adult. And this in turn is only a part of the insistent tendency of American society generally to press upon the child a premature external adulthood at the expense of the inner one: dressing the little boy like a man; setting the child before the same TV set that serves the adult; encouraging the grade school to imitate the high school and the high school to imitate the college; permitting the social relationship of early adolescents to become an imitation of marriage. Add to this the general failure of Americans to understand that the term "democracy" was intended as the description of a certain quality of political institutions, designed to prevent the abuse of the great powers of government over the life and death of the individual citizen, but that it was never supposed to constitute a "way of life" or a principle for the operation of all organizational structures of whatever nature — add this failure, and you have small reason for surprise that students, herded together on a college campus, jump to the conclusion that they ought to run the place. In these silly demands, implying as they do the total confusion of responsibility and authority, American society has the reflection of its own congenital fear and distaste for both these essentials of social existence — of its timid aversion to the idea of anyone telling anyone else, except in business or the military establishment, what to do.

A vivid example of the absurdity of such demands can be seen in the attempt of students on at least two campuses to force the university to divest itself of securities that represent investments in the South African economy. Aside from the fact that the trustees of these institutions presumably have, as fiduciaries, no right to be swayed by such things as student political opinion in the exercise of their responsibility to the financial interests of the institution, let us look for a moment at the substance of this demand.

I myself recently spent some time in South Africa, and I know of no one familiar with the situation there who does not see in the continued rapid development of the South African economy the greatest single impediment to the realization of the official concept of *apartheid* and the greatest hope, accordingly, for advancement of the country's black and "coloured" inhabitants. It is further evident that every intensification of the isolation of that country from the world community plays into the hands of the regime in its efforts to impose the policies of "separate development." Whoever is sincerely interested in the breakdown of the existing racial restrictions there ought normally to be interested in encouraging both the development of South African industry as such and the maximum participation of foreign capital in the process. Nor is there any reason to suppose that the withdrawal or denial of participation by the American investor would have the slightest effect on official South African policies. There are ample alternative sources of industrial capital, including internal ones of formidable capacity. Whatever foreign investor rejects, for ideological reasons alone, favorable possibilities for investment in that country penalizes literally no one but himself.

The agitation of the students over this issue reflects, therefore, not only a wholly improper interference in matters that are in no way their responsibility or concern but also an ignorance of the situation, and a willingness to be guided by emotional slogans and fixations, that constitute a poor recommendation for their competence as financial advisers.

The universities, obviously, have no choice but to stand their ground in the face of such demands. Many of them, it seems to me, should do it with greater firmness than they have recently exhibited. In the relationship between university and student it is, without exception, the student who is the favored party. He did not create the institution in which he is studying. He has no experience of its past, no expertise for its present, no responsibility to its future. Even if university trustees and administrators had a right to shift to him a portion of their responsibilities for the conduct of the institution, which they do not, he would be unqualified to receive it. The trustees and administrators can do no other than to establish the conditions on which and on which alone, in the interests of the effectiveness of the educational process, they can make their facilities available to the student. If the student finds these conditions unacceptable, the answer should be: no one compels him to remain there.

viii

It is superfluous to remind the reader that not just the American political system but the very organization of American life has traditionally been based on a division of responsibilities as well as of powers. The responsibility of the elector was quite a different one from that of the man he elected to office. The responsibility of the man elected to one office was not identical with that of the man elected to another. The responsibility of men banded together corporately for the transaction of commercial or industrial business was not the same as that of the government official, nor was it necessarily the same in the case of different corporations. The judge had responsibilities not shared by the legislator or by the common citizen.

In particular, certain duly elected or appointed officials, some legislative and some executive, were seen as sharing among themselves the responsibility for conducting foreign policy and making provision for the national defense. In this, they were accountable, indeed, to the electorate, but only through the formal electoral process. If, in the conduct of their office, they wandered too far from the electoral mandate or from the evolution of public opinion they could, at the appointed time, be replaced by action of a majority of the voters at the

183

polls; but so long as they were in office, the responsibility for what they did in the exercise of that office was theirs.

The responsibility of the voter, on the other hand, was substantially exhausted once he had performed his act of election. He could remain in touch with his elected representatives. He could make known to them, either through public statement or through private communication, any discontent he might feel with what they were doing. He could warn them that their persistence in a given course might cause him to vote against their re-election. But beyond this he could hardly go. Having elected them to government office, he was obliged to permit them to govern. And it was then their conscience, not his, that was engaged by the wisdom or the appropriateness of their official acts. The voter could reproach himself, if he wished, for his earlier electoral choice. He could try to expiate his mistake at the next election. But the responsibility for what the elected officials did in the exercise of their powers of office, so long as they were there, was theirs alone.

For anyone familiar with the American constitutional system, these are fairly obvious propositions; and I would not weary the reader with their repetition here if there were any indication that they were either understood or accepted by the student Left or, for that matter, by a large part of the New Left generally in this country. It is obvious that for these people the principles in question have been replaced by an opposite one which we might call "the principle of the total ubiquity of responsibility": the principle that everyone is responsible for anything, and anyone is responsible for everything. In the case of Vietnam and the draft, the connection between governmental policy and individual conscience has of course a greater plausibility than in other instances — though even here there is great confusion involving the question of the responsibility of the soldier generally for the orders of the superiors: — confusion as to whether it is war itself, as an institution; or a particular war, as a question of policy and morality of concept; or some specific abuse of the laws of war — that is at stake. But clearly, the principles on which the New Left operates do not draw the line at military operations in which the individual citizen might be asked to participate. They move on to include within the range of individual conscience situations in which the responsibility of the individual citizen could not conceivably have been engaged, or be in danger of being engaged, by any act of omission or commission on his part, for the simple reason that he is never given opportunity to influence the situation one way or another. Thus responsibility for Vietnam, in their view, goes far beyond the student who has been, or is likely to be, drafted. Each of us, it would be held, has a share of the guilt, and each of us — a share of the responsibility, for what our government is doing there. The student in Maine, by the same token, is responsible for the customs and conditions that prevail in Amite, Mississippi; and if they fail to correspond to what he, from his vantage point at a distance of two thousand miles, finds proper and acceptable, it is his business to act personally — not, mind you, through his elected representatives, but directly and in person — to set things to rights.

In one of the student letters, bitter reproach is levied at the fathers of students. Where were they, it is asked, when Adlai Stevenson lied (the charge is the letter-writer's, not mine) at the UN, when the Bay of Pigs action was in progress, when the United States "invaded" Santo Domingo? The fact that these fathers had no part, could have had no part, would not have been permitted to have any part, in the governmental processes by which these things occurred, is apparently neither here nor there. They are held responsible. They let it happen.

The concept of how this responsibility is to be acquitted is in itself interesting. The first requirement, ostensibly, is that one should "speak out," "register his dissent," "voice his protest," "refuse to remain silent." But it is plain that those who use these phrases have something more in mind than just the normal participation of the dissenter in public debates.* One should, in their view, band together demonstratively with other people. One should endeavor to shock people in government, not to persuade them. Above all, one should refuse to perform one's normal function in life, and do what one can to prevent others from performing theirs,

* I myself, for example, as noted above, have not been sparing in my public criticism of policies leading to the Vietnam war; but this, most obviously, does not absolve me from blame. There should, I gather, have been more evidences of excitement and indignation on my part — more noise and less thought.

until the government "listens" and does what one wants — not necessarily what an electoral majority in the country wants, but what one, on the basis of one's own moral feeling, sees as desirable. Failing this, one has not expurgated one's guilt; one has not cleared his conscience or met his responsibility.

And this obligation rests not just on the individual citizen; corporations, institutions, and public bodies of all sorts are also bound by it. Notwithstanding the fact that universities in other parts of the world are normally financed out of the public purse and administered under governmental rules and charters, the American university is seen as seriously remiss if it even permits research to be performed on its premises under government contract; and this — regardless of the nature of the research, regardless of whether it does or does not contribute usefully to the general fund of learning. It is remiss in doing these things because by so doing it accepts responsibility for governmental policies. The university could presumably perform work for the government without subjecting itself to reproach only if governmental policies were ones of which "we all" approved. But a government sinning in one direction can do no good, we are asked to believe, when it acts in any other. If any part of its policy is unacceptable, the totality of its action must be regarded as polluted, and rejected accordingly. The university must not, therefore, ask itself whether the immediate uses to which governmental money is being put do or do not promote those scholarly purposes to which the university is committed;

the university must sit in judgment over all major governmental policies, and if any of them do not meet with its moral approval, and more importantly with the approval of idealistic students and faculty members on campus, then it must break its ties with the government, decline money for any and all purposes, and deny the government its collaboration, even in causes that might, in themselves, be worthy.

This insistence that nothing good should be permitted to take place under governmental aegis if anything bad is also held to be taking place there has far-reaching implications. Carried to its logical conclusion, it would mean the paralysis of all useful governmental activity so long as any part of the government's action meets with the opposition of a vocal, vehement, and effectively organized minority. This has already happened in the cases of a number of highly useful and constructive things the Central Intelligence Agency was once doing. The Agency was doing them largely for the simple and innocent reason that our government structure had (and still has) no federal ministry of culture to handle matters of that sort, and it was the only governmental agency with sufficient financial and administrative flexibility to perform them. It was a question of CIA doing them or, as has since proved to be the case, their not being done at all. Perhaps it is because this sort of pressure — "you do what *we* want, or you will not be permitted to do anything at all" — has now become so familiar a feature of the American labor scene that few see objection to it when it is practiced on the wider stage of national policy. This, in any case — the deliberate paralysis of other and admittedly useful functions as a means of compelling change of governmental policy in a single direction — is exactly what the New Left want and what they specifically call for, even to the point of demanding such things as nonpayment of taxes so long as the Vietnam war is not terminated. The fact that dozens of useful and necessary functions that the government performs would be lamed if this practice became general and successful is, to the single-track mind of the political extremist for whom a single issue usually overshadows all others, only an advantage.

It is by no means only students who raise this demand for the primacy of politics over all normal functions of public, semipublic, and corporative bodies. I recently attended a National Book Awards ceremony in New York where one of the award-winners took to task, successively, his publisher — Harper and Row, the American Book Publishers Council which was giving the award, and Yale University (how Yale came into it, I cannot recall) for their respective failure to protest the Vietnam war. He then ostentatiously turned over his monetary award, on the spot, to the representative of some peace organization active in the anti-Vietnam cause. The implication, of course, was that the American Book Publishers Council had been at fault in occupying itself with such a silly thing as the recognition of literary merit when there were worthier causes to which it should have devoted its concern and its money. A large proportion of those in attendance appeared to be in enthusiastic agreement.

I was intrigued, I must say, by the rationale of this performance. I had been under the impression that it was the business of Harper and Row to publish books, of the American Book Publishers Council to represent its members in their common professional interests, and of Yale University to educate young men. To the award-winner and his followers this was evidently a naïve view, if not worse. To them, obviously, the busines of all these bodies was to sit permanently in judgment over government policies, and if they found them out of line with what they themselves thought was right and moral, then to punish the government by placing in abeyance at least some of their own chartered functions and devoting themselves primarily to the manifestation of protest until such time as the government, shaken and intimidated — we must assume — by these evidences of opposition, gave in and altered its behavior. Whether it occurred to these people that if any of these bodies made it its business to pass public judgment in this way on any one of the government's policies, such as Vietnam, it would place itself under an obligation to react thenceforth, like a Greek chorus, to every other one, lest its silence be taken as consent; and whether they realized that the directors of these various institutions, being agents and not principals, had no authority to go beyond the chartered purposes of the institutions and set themselves up as permanent review boards on the moral soundness of governmental policies I could not tell. But it was plain that in the view of the New Left the corporate conscience, like the individual one, was to assume total dimensions.

I find no less intriguing the geographic distinctions and limits that appear to govern in the application of this principle of the ubiquity of conscience. The principle is plainly national in its scope. No internal divisions of responsibility are recognized. State lines no longer mean anything at all. Each of us is responsible for what happens even in the states where we are not voters, and even if it happens within the fields reserved to the legislative powers of the state.

But if state boundaries mean nothing, national boundaries, one gathers, mean a great deal. Beyond our borders, people are at liberty to commit every sort of beastliness without any perceptible engagement of the American conscience. Internal despotism; police brutality; the massacre of great numbers of people — even on racial or tribal grounds; foreign domination; the suppression of civil rights: all these are truly reprehensible and intolerable only when they take place under American authority. Elsewhere, and particularly where they occur under Communist auspices or are practiced by people of nonwhite racial identity, they are no occasion for vocal indignation. There was nothing, for example, particularly shocking about Ho's executing his political opponents by the tens of thousands in cold blood in

191

North Vietnam; it is, however, a hideous act of international immorality for us to try to prevent him from doing the same in the South.*

I am glad, actually, that this limitation of conscience on the part of the student Left exists. How much worse it would be, after all, if we had to confess ourselves responsible for everything that anybody does *anywhere* in the world. But this leads me to wonder whether the student could not be aided — the burden of his responsibility eased and his agony of conscience reduced — if there could be some narrowing of the geographic limits to which his sense of moral responsibility extends. Just think how much easier things would be if he, like — say — his Norwegian counterpart, had only four million people about whose morality he had to worry, instead of two hundred million. Since the national boundary at

* A notable exception to this principle are the regions of Africa south of the line of the Zambezi: Rhodesia, Mozambique and Angola, and above all South Africa. To what occurs in these regions the American conscience is definitely conceived to apply. Protest is *de rigueur;* and in accordance with the principles just noted, the normal amenities of international intercourse are to be placed in abeyance (even if their general effect is a useful one) until the powers that be in these areas are brought into submission. Not even the Olympic games may take place until they, and we, correct our errors.

It is difficult to discover on what basis of principle this distinction rests. It cannot be the issue of racial integration and civil rights, for in Mozambique and Angola this is not really the issue. It cannot be the question of submission by an African territory to rule from a European center, for in the case of Rhodesia it is precisely this that is demanded. One can only conclude that one is confronted, here, with a curious and contradictory projection of deeply rooted liberal American feelings about both colonialism and racial discrimination.

which the student conscience now makes a halt is an artificial one, could not new and narrower ones be found which, though no less artificial, would ease his problem? To this, too, I shall have to return — and in a more serious vein — at a later point in this discussion.

ix

It is in the light of the characteristics I have just discussed — the ubiquity of conscience; the unwillingness to recognize any clear delineations of function and responsibility in public life; the strong feelings about the Negro problem and Vietnam; the extremely disturbing effect of the draft; the sensitivity to what is felt as sinister interference of the government with life on campus; and the demands for greater personal license and administrative authority on campus — it is in the light of all this that one must consider the most serious and potentially explosive aspect of the state of mind of the student Left, which is the attitude taken toward the political system of the country and the relationship of the individual student to that system.

If there is any one feature that unites the writers of these letters (I can think of only one partial exception), it is the rejection of the normal electoral process as a vehicle for the realization of their own ideals and objectives. A wide variety of reasons are offered for this rejection. They range all the way from the highly sophisticated Marxist view that political structures are only façades and vehicles for the power of dominant classes, and that therefore political reform could never be adequate to assure progress in the absence of drastic social change, to outbursts of a wholly childish petulance over the fact that desires voiced have not been at once acceded to by the leaders of the government. Between these extremes a number of variations of feeling make themselves evident within the general pattern of rejection of the established political structure, and it might be well to note them, *seriatim.*

There is, first of all, the very basic fact that students cannot vote until they are twenty-one and therefore feel excluded, up to that time, from the political process. This situation rankles particularly because their susceptibility to the draft begins at the age of eighteen. Their violence of feeling over this point is not materially moderated by the reflection that most of them have only a year or two to wait before attaining their majority, that they would normally attain it before completing their undergraduate career, and that during the undergraduate years they are not apt to be drafted in any case. Nor does the thought commend itself to them that the responsibility for voting ought more normally to be borne by people who have had at least some experience with the problems and responsibilities of adult life. The same pretense to a total maturity that underlies their resistance to any and all parietal rules asserts itself here in the demand that the youthful citizen should be treated precisely like the adult one; and the fact that the demand goes unsatisfied is enough to condemn the political system and to exclude it as a possible vehicle for political change. "Do you honestly believe," I am asked by a student from Vermont, "that there is any democracy for today's student?"

Secondly, there is a feeling of bitter frustration over the fact that political demands and causes dear to the student heart are seen as not having met with response at the hands of the regular political system. Here, there is a certain differentiation in the nature of the grievance.

In some instances, there is no sign of any recognition that the electoral process and the legislative channel had anything to do with it. People appear, in these instances, to conceive of executive action as something flowing directly and exclusively from right feeling on the part of the President and his advisers or, if that right feeling is lacking, then from deference to the strongly expressed views of sizable and vocal bodies of the citizenry, not necessarily constituting a majority.

Others recognize that the electoral process and legislative organs would normally have a role to play, but they see in the failure of these institutions to solve certain problems flagrant proof of their inadequacy, justifying the resort to other channels of political expression. A student at Bowdoin sums up the argument of many letters when he asserts, as justification for student attitudes, that "current efforts at change have not produced anything." The New Left is emotional, writes a lady from Ohio, "because of the wrongs they see surrounding them, wrongs which a 'senile' Congress refuses to correct, which it often refuses even to see." "Where constitutional means fail," asks a writer from New York, "what then?"

It is characteristic of all these pleas of frustration that the causes in question, on which the electoral system fails to give satisfaction, are seen as absolutes. Either the worthiness of these causes is assumed to be obvious to any right-minded person; or the fact that they represent matters of conscience to a large body of the citizenry is seen as unchallengeable proof of their desirability. Particularly is this true with respect to Vietnam. The war there is seen as the product of a malicious persistence by the Administration in pressing forward with something which everybody knows, or should know, ought to be stopped. The very fact that it can do this — can get away with it — is proof that the system itself is faulty. Under a sound system, this could not happen. The task of the system is not to determine what causes are worthy (that we all know) but to press successfully forward to the realization of those causes whose worthiness has been accepted by us, the idealistic and right-thinking minority, as unquestionable.

"The President," one letter-writer complains, "is no longer listening to critics of his policy." "When the President of the United States," writes another, "can remain so adamant in a decision that has virtually split the nation in half, there can be no doubt that our democratic system of government is not functioning correctly." The democratic process, says another, "is being made a shambles by the war in Vietnam." Through all these voices

196

runs the thought that the very conduct of the Vietnam war, regardless of its outcome, stands as proof that one cannot reasonably look to the workings of the traditional system of representative government to meet the most pressing needs of our society.

There is another group of my correspondents who feel, or seem to feel, that the existing system might conceivably cope with these major problems if it were given sufficient time, but that the problems are too urgent — they cannot wait. "The issues of the day are so important," writes a student from M.I.T., "that one cannot, in good conscience, wait years before attempting to make the Administration listen to one's views." "There must be time," a Yale senior argues,

for the education of the electorate, there must be time for democratic process, and there must be time for institutional evolution. And today, Mr. Kennan, there is no time. The urgency of the problem is incalculable.

These pleas of impatience are generally buttressed, of course, by references to the Vietnam conflict, the Negro ghetto, and the proliferation of atomic weapons; and it is not to deny the very real urgency of these problems to point out that there is a reflection here of something that is peculiarly a quality of this present younger generation: namely, the belief in, and the insistence on, an immediate, instantaneous relationship between cause and effect — between volition and action. "Everything about us," writes a neighbor — a graduate student at Princeton,

*stresses instantaneousness of gratification of wants. We
can travel anywhere in a matter of hours or days. We
can communicate instantly, get entertained instantly,
etc. . . . Is it any wonder that young people living in
this climate want instant spiritual fulfillment, instant
physical gratification, instant change in the political and
social system? Not only do these people not have the
capacity . . . for hard work towards rational goals but
they do not even have the patience for the long, hard
meditation of the Asian mystic and they take L.S.D. as a
seeming short-cut.*

A number of my correspondents, again, would accept
the existing political system, one gathers, if they could
believe it was truly representative, but they cannot. They
see it as "unresponsive to the needs of the people," "outside of morality." Politicians are "self-perpetuating";
they "do not really represent anyone except themselves
and their changing desires."

Others — more thoughtful ones, in my opinion —
concede to the system a certain representative quality,
but are suspicious generally of electoral majorities. The
reasons for the suspicion vary. Most common is the view
that the majority, given its head, has a tendency to mis-
treat, and take advantage of, minorities. "For us,"
writes a Notre Dame student, "the essence of democracy
is not the willingness to accept the dictates of the majority, but the readiness to respect and defend the dignity
and the rights of many minorities." This view is re-
iterated, in almost identical words, in other letters.

Particularly strong is the feeling that proper treatment of minorities can be extorted from the majority only by violent action, bypassing the normal political process. Here again, the note of frustration comes to the fore. "The learned professor" (meaning me), writes a gentleman in New York, "must really have been isolated in his ivory tower chambers to believe that minorities can *rely* on constitutional means to redress their injustices." "How much progress would have been made," it is asked, again, "in the civil rights movement, in educational reform, in the growth of a substantial Vietnam protest movement without the initiative of these rebels?" "In a capitalist society," says another one, "labor won its power through bloodshed. The Negro never arrived on the American scene because they [sic] never fought for their inalienable rights." For these reasons, the will of the majority cannot be regarded as "the essence of democracy." The essence of democracy is, "among other things, respect for the rights of minorities and individuals." People like Kennan who demand respect for the electoral process are really asking, writes one young man, for "mob rule by parliamentary procedure."

But the most thoughtful and telling of the voices raised against majority rule are those that charge it with a tendency to deliver up society, by perfectly legal means, to some sort of dictatorship or despotism. Appeal is sometimes taken, here, to Thomas Jefferson and his views on revolution. It is also pointed out repeatedly, and not without justification, that Adolf Hitler came into power by legal means. "Is it not true," asks a troubled and very thoughtful Albany clergyman, "that men usually lose their liberties legally? . . . Personally, I fear the loss of our liberties through a descent into fascism in strict accordance with law far more than I fear the protesting 'lawlessness' of our youth."

There is an old-American flavor to these fears of majority rule. Majorities are not to be trusted. They are apt to resign their powers to the tyrant. Minorities are different. Minorities are to be the favored children of society. They are to be protected in their rights. But they are not — one gathers — to be asked to bear responsibilities. They are to have privileges, but no duties.

In all of this, one senses not so much a fear directed to the question as to *where* governmental power is to reside, but rather a fear of such power itself — an insistence on its fragmentation in the interests of its harmlessness — a determination not to see it gathered, unified, and made real, even in the hands of an electoral majority.

This view, coming as it does from part of the New Left, has curious aspects. For one thing, it is a traditional conservative view of long standing and respectability, firmly rooted in Burke and Gibbon — one for which even I (of all people) have sympathy. It surprises me to see it emerging from a body of opinion so rife in other respects with the most exuberant Jacobinism. But beyond this, one is obliged to note that these same people who are so suspicious of the will of the majority here at home, and so determined that it shall be kept in its place, are the ones who show the most uncritical enthusiasm for the immediate establishment of "majority rule" in the countries of the southern part of the African continent. It is apparently only white majorities that are seen to have these dangerous tendencies.

There is, finally, among the reasons for rejection of the ordinary electoral process, a view of the political system that sees it all, executive and legislative alike, as wholly oppressive, brutal, conspiratorial, inaccessible to the collaborative influence of right-minded people, indistinguishable, in fact, from that of Nazi Germany or other examples of extreme despotic rule. The usual reason given for this view is the violence done by the government in drafting students and forcing them either to fight in a war they regard as immoral, or go to prison. But there are also numerous passages suggesting that students see themselves as the victims of a regime determined to suppress them in their right of freedom of speech and in their civil rights generally. In this, little or no distinction is made between the right to speak and the right to be heeded: the fact that other people do not do what one wants is interpreted as in itself repressive. Beyond that, no effort is made to distinguish between normal means and channels of persuasion in public discussion, and efforts to force society to take cognizance of demands by disturbing the peace or interfering with normal governmental or social functions. "We intend," writes one young lady from Barnard College, "to demonstrate in a way that government can neither applaud nor fail to notice. . . . We want to cause discomfort among the apathetic because we want to cause change. [We want] to shock people like Mr. Kennan out of their smugness." A leader of the S.D.S. movement describes the efforts of himself and his associates as "creative disruption." Possible targets, he writes (in a communication *not* intended for me but for his comrades in rebellion), "include National Services offices, ROTC, hopelessly biased history and social science classes, and business school. Possible tactics should include sit-ins, mill-ins, disruption of classes, and a general student strike." It is, in many cases, precisely the suppression by the authorities of activities of this nature, or resistance to them, that is offered, in the student letters, as proof of the denial of the right of free speech. One detects in this, as in student rebellion of all times and ages, a studied disregard for the distinction between what, in the repressive action of established authority, is truly gratuitous and oppressive and what is merely an unavoidable response to student provocation.

x

The last of these propositions — that the government in Washington is an oppressive one, along totalitarian lines — seems to me not worth serious discussion. I can derive only amusement from the spectacle of students liberally invoking the right of free speech as a means of arguing that no such thing exists in this country. Several years of residence in both Hitler's Germany and Stalin's Russia qualify me, I think, to say that whoever speaks of the United States government of 1968 as a *totalitarian* government does not know what the word "totalitarian" means. Were it such a government, these student demonstrations and protests would not be taking place at all, and those who are now loudest in their protests would be as still as mice.

One feature of the student outlook that is worth comment is the absence of any visible awareness of the importance of an independent and impartial judiciary in the framework of our political system. This strikes me particularly because it represents so sharp a contrast to my own view of political institutions. Had anyone asked me in recent years which of the foundations of democratic government — the elected executive, the elected legislature, or the independent judiciary — I would least like to part with, or which, if we could have only one of the three, I would most like to retain, I would unhesitatingly have decided for the judiciary. It is better, as I see it, to live under bad laws fairly and impartially administered than to live under good ones for the proper application of which no adequate judicial sanction exists, just as it is better to have narrower rights guaranteed by independent courts than wider ones against the arbitrary denial or curtailment of which there is no judicial recourse. It is not an insignificant fact that during the madness attendant, in the 1940's and early 1950's, on the activities of the late Senator Joseph McCarthy, the only branch of the government that remained substantially unaffected was the judiciary. The Senator's weapon against his victims was the deprivation, or threat of deprivation, of reputation — a punishment which, owing to his own position and the powers generally of congressional committees, he was often able to inflict without involving the law or the courts. Any victim who could contrive to bring his case before a court was, as a rule (there were exceptions), assured of protection. Of all of this, I see in the student letters no sign of recognition; and I am obliged, once again, to wonder what has been wrong with the teaching of politics in this country, that such a gap in understanding should exist.

To the charge that our electoral system is not adequately representative, I can only agree. Control over the process of nomination by professional party machines; the power of interest groups and lobbies (particularly, today, the unions) standing outside of any framework of formal responsibility; the vast bulk, weight and momentum of the military-industrial complex, as pointed to by President Eisenhower at the time he left office: all of these do indeed interfere seriously with the relationship that ought to exist between the electorate and the legislative process. It was precisely for this reason that I urged the student Left, in the Swarthmore speech, to direct its attention more to the structural reform, and less to the policies, of government. I thought the words I used in this connection were clear enough. "If the student Left," I said,

had a program of constitutional amendment or political reform — if it had proposals for the constructive adaptation of this political system to the needs of our age

204

. . . then many of us . . . could view its protests with respect . . .

Very few of the student correspondents appear to have understood what I was talking about when I used these words. Time after time, in the letters, their views on desirable changes of governmental *policy* were thrown up to me as refutation of the suggestion that they did not have a program for structural change in, or reform of, our political institutions. This difference between a change of *structure* and a change of *policy* — between the *institutions* of government, on the one hand, and what I referred to as the *"workings"* of those institutions, on the other — seemed to escape them entirely. I can see in this only another manifestation of the dreadful confusion that prevails in their thinking about political institutions generally, and particularly of their tendency to view government as some sort of force outside of society — as the master, rather than the product, of the political institutions by which the country lives.

That minorities should have protection from the tyranny of the majority is something nobody would deny. But this does not seem to me to be a danger that is particularly acute in our country, where the traditional system of government rests largely on the veto power of individual minorities and interest groups. It is hard, in fact, to think of any system, unless it be that of the Swiss, which has done better in protecting the interests of minorities. Where American minorities have been oppressed or unjustly treated, it has most often been not the will of the national majority, even as filtered through the corrupting influence of the political machinery, but rather the power of other minorities, social or sectional, that has been at fault. The Southern whites, too, we must remember, are a minority. Are their feelings and interests also to be respected? No, would say the spokesmen of the New Left. Why not? Because they are immoral and unjust. All right, but this then pits the opinion of one minority as to what is just and moral against that of another. If we are to decide these issues on a national, rather than a sectional scale (which I am not, at this point advocating, but which is, surely, the accepted theory of the New Left itself), then who is to strike the balance, if not the national majority?

That there is a possibility, finally, of the consignment by a majority of the liberties of the population into the hands of some non-democratic force is also something I would not for a moment dispute. For years, Gibbon's dictum "Under a democratical government the citizens exercise the powers of sovereignty; and those powers will be first abused, and afterwards lost, if they are committed to an unwieldy multitude" has lain at the heart of my political philosophy. But surely, the best sanctions against this eventuality will be found in the preservation of a strong and independent judiciary and in the vitality of the parliamentary process itself, and least of all in any direct interaction between the broad mass of the citizenry, or individual elements of it, and an all-powerful executive.

Every legislative body is in many respects an evil;

but it is a necessary one. It provides worse government, unquestionably, than does a benevolent despotism. But it provides better government than the non-benevolent despotism into which the benevolent one has a tendency eventually to evolve. The parliamentary institution, imperfect as it is, stands as a wholly indispensable link between the will of the people and the execution of supreme governmental authority. Where it does not exist at all, as in late nineteenth century Russia, or where it begins to lose vitality and authority, as is to some extent the case in our own country today, there is trouble ahead. This is why it is so important to think about the ways in which our own electoral and legislative system could be improved, and so futile to attempt to bypass this question entirely as one thinks of changes one would like to see made in governmental policy.

xi

The rejection, or disregard, by radical students of the traditional American political process raises the question as to what they conceive as the alternative to it. Strangely enough, contemptuous as most of them are of the system as a means of political self-expression, I find very few signs of any desire to do away with it entirely. The California youth, just cited, who described his purpose as "creative disruption," did indeed mention, in the latter part of his paper, certain things as being necessary "if we ever expect to take power." There are occasional references in other letters and statements to "revolution," but these often appear to relate to something conceived as being already in process. ("Man, revolution is already what we have in the cities, and you don't seem to know it.") One wonders whether those who use the term "revolution" this way really know what it traditionally means. That it means, in their minds, to defy power is clear; but that it means to replace power, and above all, to shoulder responsibilities that go with it, is not clear at all.

The nearest thing to a coherent formulation of what is supposed to come in the place of what we now have is the call of certain of the elements of the New Left for "participatory democracy." The most explicit definition of the term that I have encountered is that given by Mr. Newfield, in his work *A Prophetic Minority*, already referred to (page 141, note). He defines it as

the notion that ordinary people should be able to affect all the decisions that control their lives. The idea that social reformation comes from organizing the dispossessed into their own insurgent movements rather than from forming top-down alliances between liberal bureaucratic organizations. The insistence on fraternity and community inside the movement. The passion against manipulation and centralized decision-making. The reluctance to make the New Left itself a machine tooled and fueled to win political power in the traditional pit battles.

"Decentralism, communitarianism, and existential humanism" are, he goes on to say, the definite qualities of the New Left. And he describes the forebears of the movement as "the Whitman–Emerson–Thoreau transcendentalists, and the Joe Hill–Bill Hayward Wobblies."

Well, these are clues, to some extent informative. But they still fail to answer the question: what, when this movement of "participatory democracy" has ripened, achieved its full strength, put all the rest of us to shame, and emerged triumphant — what then becomes of the President, and Congress, and the Constitution? Inadequate they are, we understand, and deserving only of scorn and suspicion. But no one has yet suggested they be wholly done away with, nor have I as yet detected any ideas as to what would take their place in case they were. Not one of the many letters has thrown any light on this question.

One is left with a strong impression that these agencies of bureaucracy and imperialism are to remain in existence and to continue to bear the heavy responsibility of government, but that they are merely to be provided, henceforth, with a new and much more painful thorn in their side, in the form of a powerful New Left.

I find it difficult, frankly, to picture the reality of this dream. If the system remains unchanged, it must logically be expected to continue to throw up into positions of high governmental responsibility just such people (in the student view: reprehensible characters — selfish, reactionary, corrupt, devoid of vision) as now man the senior echelons of government. Left to themselves, these deplorable characters would continue, we must assume, to follow the same intolerable policies, to make themselves guilty of the same evasions and omissions. It is true that they are not to be left unmolested. From now on, they are to be plagued by the New Left — a New Left grown in popular strength, unwithstandable in its righteousness and anger, but constituting still the political expression not of the people as a whole but only of "the dispossessed," who are, after all, a minority. Under the pressure of this minority faction, the President and his advisers are to be pushed, reluctantly and gnashing their teeth, one must assume, from one constructive action to another, each contrary to their own wishes and contrary to, or at least not included in, their electoral mandate.

My correspondents, in pressing this view upon me, have confronted me with many rhetorical questions. I can now only reply with one of my own. Does anyone seriously believe that the process of government could effectively work this way? The task of conducting the affairs of a great nation in the modern age is hard enough in any event — hard enough even when those who bear the responsibility are supported by active faith and confidence and enthusiasm for what they are doing. Can it really be supposed that a government such as ours could function successfully in the manner just suggested: staggering clumsily and reluctantly along like a stubborn, rebellious donkey, beaten and goaded into sporadic lurches along paths it does not wish to pursue?

This idea has, to be sure, respected roots in the American political tradition. It was the favored concept of the many professional "needlers" of the end of the last century and the beginning of this one: the reformers, the muckrakers, the peace enthusiasts, the unrelenting gadflies who in 1927–1928 maneuvered the unfortunate Mr. Kellogg into the absurdity of his universal pact for the outlawry of war. All of these people saw their function in life as that of kicking an unenlightened government into the adoption of measures for which it had neither desire nor understanding.

I am bound to say that as a historian, I found this concept reprehensible even in terms of an earlier age. Now, as one who has imprudently allowed himself to be lured into current political controversy, I find it equally faulty. It is not that there is no place in our political life for the challenging and stimulating influence of an idealistic, progressive and determined minority, but there is no place for it as a purely critical, irresponsible, and politically unorganized force, attempting to act directly on an Executive for which it has no respect and to which it sees no alternative. To be effective in its quality as a movement of protest and reform, such a minority must accept the responsibility of confronting the electorate at the polls. It must look to the affirmative understanding of the electorate, not to the reflexes of a frightened and bewildered Executive, for the realization of its ideals. The problem is not how to make a bad system work well by abusing it; the problem is to change it in such a way that it will work well without abuse.

One cannot suffer exposure to these views of the student Left without being impressed with the extent to which they reflect those that were expressed by Thoreau in his essay on "Civil Disobedience." Many of the students were themselves familiar with this essay and referred specifically to it in their letters; but I think the influence goes far beyond anything that many of them are conscious of.

In a sense, this is not surprising. The parallels between their concerns and those of Thoreau at the time when he wrote this essay, are quite startling. He, like them, had two causes on his mind: the mistreatment of the American Negro, and the prosecution by the United States government of what he regarded as an unjust war on the territory of another country (the war with Mexico). In neither case could he reconcile the existing state of affairs with the dictates of his own conscience as a citizen. His view, like that of his contemporary sympathizers, was essentially anarchical in its implications. He did not call for the immediate abolition of all government, but he looked to this abolition as the ultimate goal. He, too, did not question the correctness of his own judgment of what was right and what was wrong. He, like his followers of this day, looked to government to accept his judgment as the point of departure and to give it immediate reality. Like them, he had no respect for the majority. He, too, saw in the majority a danger to the rights of the minority. He was content that government should continue to decide issues in which the element of conscience was not involved; but where it was involved, the issues could not be resigned to the legislator. "After all," he wrote, "the practical reason why . . . a majority are permitted, and for a long period continue, to rule is not because they are most likely to be right, nor because this seems fairest to the minority, but because they are physically the strongest." And he, too, was impatient. He did not believe that men "ought to wait until they have persuaded the majority" before attempting to change unjust laws. "The ways which the state has provided for remedying the evil" were not for him. "They take too much time," he wrote, "and a man's life will be gone." He, too, repudiated the government's representative quality, and spurned the idea that one should recognize it as the vehicle for his self-assertion as a citizen, or give it his respect and obedience. "How," he asked, "does it become a man to behave toward this American government to-day? I answer, that he cannot without disgrace be associated with it. I cannot for an instant recognize that political organization as *my* government which is the slave's government also." Voting, therefore, was not enough. "Even voting *for the right* is *doing* nothing for it. It is only expressing to men feebly your desire that it should prevail." He, too, accordingly, took refuge in the concept of direct action by the people — participatory democracy, if you will.

One hears in Thoreau's words the true inspiration of the feelings of young people of our day, faced again, as he was, with the demand for their support of a war they regard as unjust, and with the unmistakable evidence of the failure of American society to provide in its midst a dignified and hopeful place for the Negro citizen.

These deep roots in Thoreau's thought represent, to me, the most impressive aspect of the entire outlook of the student Left; for the history of American political thought contains no more moving and noble vision of individual freedom than Thoreau's great essay. And yet . . . Thoreau's words and actions were an embarrassment to his more prominent and influential friends in the abolitionist movement — men whose voices were at that time more important to the advancement of the cause than his own. His essay, far from solving, never even faced the question of whose view was to prevail when the dictates of conscience conflicted as between one individual or another, between one minority or another, or between the conscience of an individual and the collective conscience of men charged with the responsibilities of government, men whose choices were more complex than those of any individual, and who like the trustees of Columbia University had to consider themselves as agents, not principals. Nor did his view stand up very well against the specific realities of the situations he had in mind. The war with Mexico was terminated, and not as a result of any widespread civil disobedience, before the ink was fairly dry on his essay. And as for slavery: twelve years later the federal government did indeed proceed along the lines he advocated, and took armed action against the South in the interests of the eventual abolition of slavery. Not only did it take the action, but it was, in the military and formal sense, successful. Yet here, today, one hundred and twenty years later, are thousands of young men just as upset about the situation of the American Negro in this country as Thoreau was then. To me, this suggests that the problem is much more complex, more deeply rooted and less susceptible to solution by simple and immediate measures than Thoreau supposed. Could this not be just as true of his present followers?

xiii

Here, then, is today's radical student. He is, as he might be expected to be in an overwhelmingly urban society, a distinctly urban creature. He is anxious, angry, humorless, suspicious of his own society, apprehensive with relation to his own future. Overexcited and unreflective, lacking confidence in anyone else, impatient and accustomed to look for immediate results, he fairly thirsts for action. Romantic and quixotic, he is on the prowl for causes. His nostrils fairly quiver for the scent of some injustice he can sally forth to remedy. Devoid of any feeling for the delineation of function and responsibility, he finds all the ills of his country, real or fancied, pressing on his conscience. He is not lacking in courage: he is prepared, in fact, to charge any number of windmills. But in doing so he is often aggressive and unintentionally destructive toward what he needs to live by, destructive sometimes toward himself.

What makes him this way? Certain of the causes are

215

external, temporary and relatively superficial. I have already mentioned the devastatingly unsettling effect of Vietnam and the draft. But underlying the very intensity with which he reacts to these things, there are obviously far deeper, and largely subconscious, sources of discomfort.

He is the product of his national culture and his time. He reflects faithfully, but in expanded, oversized dimensions, like shadows on the wall, the bewilderments and weakness of parents, teachers, employers, molders of opinion, leaders of government. He comes, often, from a home that is affluent yet insecure. He senses in his parents, and feels in himself, the malaise of material satiety without the balancing influence of any inner security. Imagination, fears, hopes, desires: all these are overstimulated, and prematurely stimulated, by exposure to the products of the commercialized mass media. Yet there are no adequate countervailing sources of strength, confidence and hope. There is no strong and coherent religious faith, no firm foundation of instruction in the nature of individual man, no appreciation for the element of tragedy that unavoidably constitutes a central component of man's predicament, and no understanding for the resulting limitations on the possibilities for social and political achievement. The student is the victim of the sickly secularism of this society, of the appalling shallowness of the religious, philosophic and political concepts that pervade it. And in addition to all this, his estrangement from nature, his intimacy with the machine, his familiarity with the world of gadgetry, and his total lack of understanding for the slow powerful processes of organic growth, all these imbue him with an impatience and an expectation of an immediate connection between stimulus and effect that do not fit even with the realities of his own development as a person, and even less with those of the development of a society.

As a result of this complex of formative influences, the student suffers at college age from the effects of an extreme disbalance in emotional and intellectual growth. In certain ways he is precocious and over-mature. In other ways he is much more childlike than were students of an earlier and simpler age. Between these extremes of over- and underdevelopment a tension is created which causes him acute unease, while the origins of it largely escape his consciousness. It is from this that there flows the frantic, anxious, troubled nature of his behavior. It renders him ill-prepared to meet the demands on his patience that the slow process of educational growth inevitably imposes. For this reason, while his unhappiness could certainly be greatly alleviated by the removal of Vietnam and the draft as aggravating factors, this would still not really solve the problem, as he would himself search for others to take their place. His misery has its roots in the society out of which he emerged, and it can be entirely cured only in the sanification of that society itself.

When the roots of a problem run as deep as this, and when they lie in something as slow and deep-seated as the development of an entire society, it is obvious that the remedies must in the main be long-term ones, calculated for the decades rather than for the years. I shall refer to some of these in the final section of these comments. But this does not mean that nothing at all can be done in the short term; and this, too, deserves a word or two of comment.

There are those who will say nothing needs to be done. "Just wait awhile," they will say, "and this troubled student will be thirty. Then he will be all right." Obviously, there is something in this.

Others will say: "There have always been radical students. There always will be. They are a normal mutation of the student species." And this view, too, will have much to commend it.

But I cannot agree that these reflections give ground for complacency. The disaffection of the contemporary American student activist, like that of the nineteenth-century Russian populist student whom he so closely resembles, goes well beyond the normal, beyond the healthy, beyond what is safe for society itself. Lacking the balance of a sense of humor, lacking perspective on itself, saturated with scorn for the political system yet devoid of all but the most childish ideas as to how that system could be improved, this state of mind takes the form of an embittered pseudo-revolutionary nihilism — a nihilism not, for the moment, dangerous in itself, but pernicious in its effect on the campus atmosphere generally, and pregnant with possibilities for real mischief if not checked and moderated. It serves to confuse the minds of other students less inclined temperamentally to such bitter and antisocial attitudes. And it could become definitely dangerous if it were to be captured by, or to enter into combination with, a political force more mature, more purposeful, better organized and more conspiratorial than itself.

Happily for us, this last danger has not yet materialized. To be sure, the student Left (particularly the S.D.S.) has been extensively influenced by Marxist-Communist stereotypes. The idea of the elusive, menacing, dimly visible "power structure," for example, is a classic Marxist image. But a number of factors, including the present disarray of the international Communist movement, the obvious role of the Soviet Union as a great imperialist power in Eastern Europe, the example of student unrest in Russia itself and in other Communist countries, and finally the strongly anarchical spirit, resistant to all organizational discipline, that prevails in the New Left of the American campus: all these have sufficed, to date, to frustrate the development of any serious degrees of Communist organizational influence over this body of student opinion.

A political association of the radical American white student with the violent black power movement could also have seriously disturbing consequences. Such an association has apparently been obviated thus far by the simple fact that the black power leaders have so little use for the white student, however sympathetic.

But these fortunate circumstances reflect rather the momentary good fortune of American society than any deeper logic of the situation; and one cannot depend on their endurance. It was out of just such radical students, frustrated in their efforts to help the Russian peasant, that Lenin forged his highly disciplined faction. It was in part from people of just this desperate and confused state of mind that Hitler recruited his supporters. To leave a large portion of student youth in the frame of mind it is in today, aside from the fact that it deprives society generally of resources of energy, idealism and enthusiasm that it sorely needs, is always a dangerous thing.

The entity best qualified to do something about this situation in the short term is the United States government. But there are certain things that the government (and in this I include both Congress and the Executive) must face up to, if it wants to move successfully in this direction. The government must face the fact, in the first place, that it is unwise to draft, particularly for combat service, men who are not yet old enough to vote. One must either extend the franchise to men one intends to draft, or one must refrain from drafting those who do not enjoy the franchise.

Secondly, the government must recognize that it is foolish to try to conduct cruel, messy wars — wars of obscure origin and rationale, fought in theaters halfway around the world — with draftee personnel. If one cannot refrain from conducting such wars, one must do it with professional soldiers. And if there are not enough of such soldiers, one must regard this deficiency as an absolute limitation on what one can expect to do, as though it were a shortage of ships or munitions. What one must not do is to try to make up the deficiency by exposing the entire male student population of the country to an uncertainty which seriously demoralizes its members in the pursuit of their studies, and then hauls a portion of them away to a form of service they regard with fear, loathing and shame.

The best thing the government could do, when this miserable war is over, would be to revise basically the entire system governing the relationship between the young male American and his obligation of military service. There should, obviously, be a strong, well-paid, professional military arm, ready at all times to undertake those military tasks that do not grow into a general war and engage the totality of the national effort. But I wonder whether there should not be, in place of the present draft system with all its injustices and inequalities and uncertainties, a system of universal national service, to embrace all young men of a certain age, regardless of physical condition, and possibly all women as well. There is no reason why this service should be entirely military. It should no doubt include, for the men, a certain amount of basic military training; but it could certainly embrace a number of other useful functions, of a Peace Corps nature, with relation to the development of the country at large. It should come between sophomore and junior year of college, and a great many of those who complete it should not then go on to junior and senior year but should consider their formal education complete and should enter directly into the civilian labor market, thus unburdening the universities and making it possible for them to gear the last two years of undergraduate study

221

more closely into the postgraduate academic careers. This would, admittedly, split the entire work of the undergraduate colleges into a junior college level, embracing all of what would today normally be the college population, and a junior-senior and postgraduate level, embracing — I would hope — far fewer.

Under such a system, none of the uncertainty that proves today so demoralizing for the student would exist. He would know exactly what awaited him, and for how long. He could plan his future as he liked. If the government took the same pains that — say — some of the smaller European governments do to make this period of service an enjoyable and personally profitable experience for him, instead of leaving his intellectual and spiritual development while in service to the comics, the smut magazines, and the camp movies, it could be a force both for true social democratization and for training in the meaning of citizenship.

But the government, for this and other reasons, must learn how to communicate with the students. The universities, with their present inordinate size and impersonality, often fail them in this respect. The government must not fail them too. They must not be left, while in college, to the mercies of the mass media or the campus agitator. That is just asking for trouble. The government must recognize that by exposing so many young people to the stimulus of a college education, half-baked as many of these stimuli are, we have created a situation that calls for a decisive change in the tone and rhetoric of American public life. These people will no longer be content with the sort of patter that would draw applause from the crowd at the county fair. The traditional vocabulary of American politics — the hearty bombast, the banging of the chauvinistic bell, the measureless national self-congratulation, the huffy assertions of suspicion and truculence directed to the outside world, and the ritualistic invocation of a pious anticommunism to justify anything for which a more meaningful argument might seem too subtle or too difficult — this language will no longer do. One section of the public, perhaps, still wants this sort of thing. But there is now another large section, and it includes a good portion of the student youth, that will not accept it. Government has to learn to take this rejection seriously and to apply itself to the filling of the resulting gap. If this means greater humility, greater patience with other people's outlooks, greater study of their intellectual needs, and a greater respect for the very process of sophistical communication than it has been accustomed to dredging out of its smug and self-centered official soul, so be it.

The second agency that has possibilities for the short-term and partial alleviation of the unhealthy aspects of student activism is the university itself. Its problems are complex. They vary from institution to institution. I would not like to cheapen the discussion of the subject by attempts at generalization. It seems to me that by and large I have seen more harm done, in this recent period, by excessive permissiveness, and above all by lack of confidence on the part of the university in its own values and standards, than by any excess of disciplinary zeal. A stricter code for student behavior implies, admittedly, a readiness to resort fairly extensively to expulsion as means of enforcement. With this, too, I see nothing wrong. Education is a privilege, and one that presupposes certain responsibilities and self-restraints on the part of the subject; it is not an absolute right, independent of conduct. If the young person expects to enjoy this privilege, his behavior must be generally conducive to the success of the educational process itself, and certainly not destructive of it. Otherwise, he becomes an impediment not only to his own intellectual and personal growth, but to that of other students as well; and this the institution has no obligation — and indeed no right — to tolerate.

This brings me to the student himself, and to *his* possibilities for alleviating his own distress. For if he is not entirely an adult, he is also not entirely a child. He can, if he wishes, observe and think, instead of just emoting; and he is already at an age where he has some share of the responsibility for his own condition.

I said at the outset of this treatise that it would not be addressed to the students themselves. But perhaps I may attempt now, in conclusion, to sum up what I might say to a composite student activist if I had him before me and if he would listen that long. It would be something like this:

I am not as critical of you, when all is said and done, as you think. There is much to be said on your side. Our society is endangered. So is world peace. So, indeed, is

224

the very survival of *Western civilization* — in both the spiritual and physical sense. For all of this your government, and the generation which has supported that government, bear a heavy measure of responsibility. You may well have a sense of grievance over the fact that you have been propelled into such a world.

Your understanding, on the other hand, both of what it is that is wrong and of the elements of responsibility involved, is shallow and inadequate — lacking in historical depth, lacking in understanding for what the human predicament really is, lacking in appreciation for the element of tragedy in human affairs, lacking in feeling for the importance of such things as continuity, custom and familiarity as components in any process of mass adjustment to new conditions. This is why I made the suggestion that so many of you resented: that you take advantage of the opportunity you have now, at college, and will never have again, to do some studying and to deepen understanding in all these respects, so that when you do come to a responsible involvement in public affairs you will be better prepared for it. So long as your analysis of the problem is shallow, the remedies that commend themselves to you are almost bound to suffer from the same distortion, and they are not likely to be effective.

I recognize that the draft, more than any other single factor, causes you to feel that it is not you who have involved yourselves in the affairs of the government, but the government that has involved you. I concede your point, here, and give you my sympathy. I would ask you, however, not to exaggerate and over-

225

dramatize your plight. It will not be made easier by your doing so. And I think you should not make such heavy sledding of it from the standpoint of conscience. It was not you who started this war; it is not really you who can stop it. The decision is not yours, nor is the responsibility.

If you are drafted and unhappy about it, I do not think you should go to prison or flee the country. I think it would be in order for you to tell your draft board, without disrespect, that you consider this a foolish and unjust war, and that you go under protest, without enthusiasm, only as a mark of respect for what your country once was and could someday again be. But I don't think you should defy completely the decision of your government, however foolish and shortsighted, that brings you before that board. To be so lacking in patience is not fair to the country, as a political entity of nearly two hundred years' standing; it is not fair to all the people who are struggling in other, and perhaps more effective, ways for things you care about; just as Thoreau's futile gesture of spending a night by his own insistence in the little Concord jail was scarcely fair to his friends in the New England abolitionist movement who were moving in other ways, and more effective ones, to achieve the same ends, and to whom his gesture came as an unnecessary reproach and claim to moral superiority.

It is perhaps not fair to ask of you that you try to recognize in yourselves the children of a generation of people disoriented by a process of technological change

226

far too sudden and precipitous for human power of adaptation. Such a burden of self-recognition is one not usually placed upon people of your age. But you will be well advised to attempt the feat. And if you attempt it, you will draw the consequence: which will be a feeling of less anger and more sadness; of less self-righteousness and greater understanding and pity for others; of a greater patience, relaxation, resignation and good humor in the face of the ordeals and choices with which our society now confronts you.

xiv

There is one more thing I owe to my student correspondents. It is a word about my own view of the problems and tasks of our society at this time. Why do I owe it to them? Because a number of them reproached me for my own failure to lead — for my own failure to face the questions I said they should face. It is not our job, at our age, they said, to say how this society can be straightened out, to draw up programs for constitutional revision or political reform. What would *you* do? they asked. "You lead" — one of them put it.

Well, I cannot end these comments by writing another book. A large part of my life has been spent either outside this country or, if here, in the study of other countries and of international affairs. My views on foreign policy are ones that I have stated in many ways and on many occasions. I have tried not to speak much about domestic affairs, because I have not really had time to study them and there are so many people who know more about them than I do.

Because I *have* lived so long outside the country and have seen how many things are done elsewhere, but also because my roots in American life go back to an earlier and simpler and happier age, now largely superseded, I have probably suffered more than the average citizen from the things that have struck my eyes and assailed my ears as I have lived in this country and wandered about it in recent years. This American civilization of which we are all the beneficiaries and the victims is one for the future of which I have the deepest apprehensions. If the students think *they* are gloomy about the American scene, and fearful of America's future, I must tell them that they haven't seen anything yet. Not only do my apprehensions outclass theirs but my ideas of what would have to be done to put things to rights are far more radical than theirs. But my views of where the dangers lie, and of where the hand should be put to redress or avert them, is radically different from theirs.

Of course, Vietnam is a great folly and danger, and the liquidation of our involvement there is a prerequisite to almost anything constructive that one can think of in our life. Behind Vietnam, too, I am free to admit, lies the nuclear weapon, and the apocalyptic dangers it holds for everyone. Let us all pray, and do whatever is in our power to assure, that this cup passes from us. But beyond these things, as I see it, there lie dangers within ourselves, within our civilization, that cast no less threatening a cloud over the future of our society. And it is with these, in addition to Vietnam and the atom, that I am preoccupied.

What are they? I can name only a few.

There is first the question of what is happening, physically, to the natural environment necessary not only to sustain life in this country but to give it healthfulness and meaning. This is a question not just of our own once so magnificent continent, which we are treating with the blind destructiveness of the army ant; it is a question of the purity and life-sustaining quality of the seas and the global atmosphere within which this continent, and we with it, has its existence. How long can man go on over-populating this planet, destroying its topsoils, slashing off its forests, exhausting its supplies of fresh water, tearing away at its mineral resources, consuming its oxygen with a wild proliferation of machines, making sewers of its rivers and seas, producing industrial poisons of the most deadly sort and distributing them liberally into its atmosphere, its streams and its ocean beds, disregarding and destroying the ecology of its plant and insect life? Not much longer, I suspect. I may not witness the beginning of the disaster on a serious scale. But many of the students who have written me will. And let us not forget that much of the damage that has already been done is irreparable in terms of the insight and effort of any single generation. It takes eight hundred years to produce a climax forest. It will take more than that, presumably, to return the poisoned, deadened waters of Lake Michigan, on the shores of which I was born, to the level of plant and fish life and natural healthfulness

that they had at the time of my birth. And even to begin
to reverse this process will require a human society far
more conscious of its obligation to the continuity of life,
and not just the possibilities for life's immediate enjoyment, than anything we see before us today, or have seen
in the past. To make it this way will require a vast process of education, which has scarcely yet begun.

Not all of this damage, of course, could be com-
bated or remedied just within the framework of our
continent alone. But much of it could be. As the world's
greatest industrial nation, as the possessor of the largest single component of its industrial machinery, also as
its most wasteful and industrially dirty society, and finally, as the world's foremost nuclear power and one
which has yet to give any very satisfactory explanation
of the manner in which it disposes of its nuclear wastes,
we have a very special responsibility here.

I see in the preoccupations and behavior of our governmental leaders very little recognition of all this. The
paltry million or two dollars they devote to the study
and treatment of these problems is as nothing compared
to what is spent on the Vietnam conflict alone. One wonders whether men have gone mad, to spend such tremendous sums on what they consider to be the military defense of a country which is so extensively destroying the
prerequisites of its own life from within.

Well, this, first of all, preoccupies me.

Next to it I would have to put something that will
surprise most people — something that many people, in

fact, will fail utterly to understand. This is the phenomenon of American advertising, and the extent to which it has been permitted to dominate and exploit the entire process of public communication in our country. It is to me positively inconceivable that the whole great, infinitely responsible function of mass communication, including very important phases of the educational process, should be farmed out — as something to be mined for whatever profit there may be in it — to people whose function and responsibility have nothing to do with the truth — whose function and responsibility, in fact, are concerned with the peddling of what is, by definition, untruth, and the peddling of it in trivial, inane forms that are positively debauching in their effect on the human understanding. After the heedless destruction of natural environment, I regard this — not advertising as such, but the consignment to the advertiser of the entire mass communications process, as a concession to be exploited by it for commercial gain — as probably the greatest evil of our national life. We will not, I think, have a healthy intellectual climate in this country, a successful system of education, a sound press, or a proper vitality of artistic and recreational life, until advertising is rigorously separated from every form of legitimate cultural and intellectual communication — until advertisements are removed from every printed page containing material that has claim to intellectual or artistic integrity and from every television or radio program that has these same pretensions, from every roadside and every bit of countryside that purports to offer to the traveler a glimpse of what his continent once was and once might be.

Is it a revolution I am demanding? Yes — a revolution in the financing and control of the process of communication generally. And if this revolution brings in the government as a replacement for the advertiser in many of these processes, I still wish for it. The government's commitment and conscience as an educator — its commitment to truthfulness and integrity in communication — may not be all that we could want. But it has at least *some* responsibility here to the public weal, and *some* obligation to keep in mind the public needs. This is more than one can say about the advertiser.

Thirdly, I worry about the private automobile. It is a dirty, noisy, wasteful, and lonely means of travel. It pollutes the air, ruins the safety and sociability of the street, and exercises upon the individual a discipline which takes away far more freedom than it gives him. It causes an enormous amount of land to be unnecessarily abstracted from nature and from plant life and to become devoid of any natural function. It explodes cities, grievously impairs the whole institution of neighborliness, fragmentizes and destroys communities. It has already spelled the end of our cities as real cultural and social communities, and has made impossible the construction of any others in their place. Together with the airplane, it has crowded out other, more civilized and more convenient means of transport, leaving older people, infirm people, poor people and children in a worse situation than they were a hundred years ago. It continues to lend a terrible element of fragility to our civilization, placing us in a situation where our life would break down completely if anything ever interfered with the oil supply.

That the internal combustion engine and the motor vehicle are here to stay, is clear. But I think much could be done to bring this means of transportation under control: to restrict its use, to limit the amount of damage it can do, to fit it into a rational system of transportation where it would have its place but would not crowd everything else out. To do even this will take something in the nature of a technological counterrevolution; but I cannot conceive of the recovery of peace and quiet and clean air and sound community relationships without it. Again, the start has yet to be made. With every year that passes, the malorganization of our life, flowing from this cause, becomes worse, and the cost and difficulty of an eventual counterrevolution become greater.

I share with almost everybody else in this country a great concern about the state of the American Negro. I regard it as our greatest social and political problem. I do not deceive myself that I have the answers to this problem. In the immediate sense I doubt that there are any decisive answers. I see the possibilities for progress (and have long seen them this way) much less in the concepts of integration — much less in the possibility of creating a homogenized society — than in some sort of a voluntary segregation and autonomy for large parts of the Negro community. In this I find that I have, to my surprise, a bond with many of the advocates of "black power," for whose methods and spirit I have in other respects nothing but abhorrence.

I do not consider that integration should be ruled out. I do not feel that we should discourage or reject it for that part of the Negro community that wants it. But I suspect that there is a considerable part of that community that does not; and I think that provision should be made, in each case, for them, as well as for the others. That this would mean helping great portions of the Negro population to remove from the big-city ghettos and freeing for them areas where they can live their own life, under their own administration, with better prospects for employment and health, I can well conceive. That all of this would take great imagination and vigor of governmental action, as well as great expense, strikes me as obvious, and not a compelling argument against it.

As for the political system: I am no specialist — no student of our political structure. I believe that our country is too large for its own good. Great countries, I think, are a menace to themselves and everyone else. People are not meant to live in such vast, impersonal political communities. Many of the evils of our life are connected, it seems to me, with the decay of the vitality of the state government — with the failure of the state government to play the part envisaged for it by our Constitution. But if the competence of the federal government is too large to permit intelligent and effective attention to be given to many problems, that of the state government is too narrow. I think we need a bold redrawing of state boundaries, particularly where they intersect great urban areas. But in addition to this I suspect that we need a breakdown of the country into a few major regions, and the creation of new regional organs of government, standing between the state and federal governments and taking over a part of the functions of both. By this decentralization I would hope that we could restore a greater intimacy to the political process, stimulate and encourage the growth of a healthy regional feeling and independence of action, reduce the bloated monstrosity and impersonality of the federal government, and permit people to concentrate, as citizens, on the problems that are near and understandable to them, instead of burdening their consciences with what takes place in remote parts of the country, the problems of which they poorly understand.

Beyond this, I suspect (I keep saying "suspect" because these are problems to which I have not been able to give serious study, and I know no more about them than does the average citizen) that there are reforms of the federal political process that are long overdue. I should think we could improve materially the process of nomination: wresting it from the hands of the professional political machines and bringing it closer to the people. It seems to me high time that we tackled the problem of the committee seniority system in Congress, and gave more careful study to the question as to whether we could not have some modified form of responsible government, on the British pattern. I wonder whether we could not do more than we have done to reduce the cost of running for public office, to bring it within the range of the average income, and to give an assured financial future to legislators, in order that they should not have to have this on their minds while they occupy themselves with the great problems of national policy.

These are all examples of the sort of thing that I, personally, worry about, dream about, hope for, or regard as the least unfavorable of given sets of alternatives, when I think about American domestic affairs. I could mention others, but these will suffice. They are identical only in small degree with things that the students have similarly in mind. But they are not less radical. Many people, in fact, will laugh at them. So "far out" are they, in their way, that merely in mentioning them here I am laying myself open, I know, to the sort of misunderstanding that so often dogged my footsteps when I was in government, and particularly when I was a planner — misunderstandings resulting from the fact that things desirable, essential, or even unavoidable in the long run often sound absurd, utopian, or just plain crazy, when placed in relation to the attitudes and possibilities of the present day.

But how, then, the skeptical but curious student will ask, do you propose to go about realizing your views? What have you done to make them reality?

Very little, is the answer. I have had other things to do in life. Not everyone can do everything. In general,

I have supposed that there could be no use at all trying to give practical advancement at this stage to thoughts so far from anything familiar to present opinion. Being a writer and a teacher, I have felt that the best I could do would be to try to explain, in the proper way and at the proper time, the reasons why I hold these views. I have been trying to do this in what is admittedly the slow way: primarily in a long intellectual autobiography, of which one volume has appeared. This is, so to speak, a tangential approach: but I think that thoughts and views are often better understood, and commend themselves better to others, when they are revealed in the context of the broader pattern of experience and personality of which they form a part than when one states them boldly and directly. This is perhaps why I react so negatively to the idea of just shouting one's views at people, or waving oversimplified placard slogans before them from the ranks of street demonstrations. I don't think ideas make their progress that way. Fears do, perhaps — likewise emotions, jealousies and resentments — but not ideas.

I have hoped that my thoughts and gropings, once they have been exposed to the attention of the reading public, would pass — as indeed the Swarthmore speech is now passing — through the refining process of public discussion, and that they would emerge from it corrected, enriched, cleansed of much of the dross that now undoubtedly clings to them.

And how, then, would I hope to see them eventually achieve realization — achieve it, that is, against what would certainly be the resistance of the professional political machines and the great established political parties?

Here, perhaps, is where I differ most strongly from my student correspondents. They would try to realize *their* political aspirations by direct, demonstrative pressure on the Administration of the moment, bypassing the electoral and legislative process. I would consider essential to the realization of *my* aspirations — and theirs, too, for that matter — the creation of a new political party, a party that would differ from the two great existing ones in the fact that it would be content to remain a minority, that it would not consider itself a failure if it did not win national elections and come into power, that it would place ideas and convictions ahead of electoral success, that it would make it its business to educate others, but to do so precisely by means of a vigorous participation in the regular political and electoral process of the country. I think it possible that such a party, not just *despite* the fact that it did not make the conquest of power the sole and overriding goal of its activities, but primarily *because* of that very fact, would eventually cut through the great professional political parties, which try to be all things to all men, like a knife through cheese.

But, the students will say, this is too slow. What you are talking about will take years. By that time, we will all be dead.

As usual, they exaggerate. I shall be dead. They probably will not. I do not think it my business, in any case, to ask whether there is time for all this, or whether there is not. The outcome is in higher hands than mine. It is here, at the end, admittedly, but at a most crucial and central point, that the Christian faith has its part. I do what I can, in my own way, and with as much fidelity as I can muster to my own nature and my own values. This, it seems to me, is the best that men can ever hope to do; for they see only dimly, their justice is imperfect, and they do not really know what is right and what is wrong. They know only whether they have done their best.

The student way is different from mine. All right — it takes all sorts to make a world. Perhaps it will some day be shown that these two ways, seemingly in conflict, have enriched each other, as conflicting human forces so often do, and that in doing so they have produced something a little better, and a little stronger, than what either originally was. If so, then both will have justified their conception and their assertion.